REAL ESTATE LAW
FOR
THE HOMEOWNER & BROKER

2nd Edition

by
Margaret C. Jasper

Oceana's Legal Almanac Series
Law for the Layperson

2000
Oceana Publications, Inc.
Dobbs Ferry, New York

Library of Congress Cataloging-in-Publication Data

Jasper, Margaret C.
   Real estate law for the homeowner and broker / by
Margaret C. Jasper.—2nd ed.
       p. cm.— (Oceana's legal almanac series. Law for the layperson)
   Includes bibliographical references.
   ISBN 0-379-11345-7 (acid-free paper)
     1. Real property—United States—Popular works.
   2.Vendors and purchasers—United States—Popular works.
   3.Real estate business—Law and legislation—United
States—Popular works.
     I. Title. II. Series.

   KF665.Z9 J37 2000
   346.7304'3—dc21

                                                    00-56660

Oceana's Legal Almanac Series: Law for the Layperson
ISSN 1075-7376

©2000 by Oceana Publications, Inc.

To My Husband Chris

Your love and support
are my motivation and inspiration

-and-

In memory of my son, Jimmy

Table of Contents

CHAPTER 2:
THE ROLE OF THE REAL ESTATE BROKER

CHAPTER 3:
BUYING AND SELLING REAL ESTATE

CHAPTER 4:
THE REAL ESTATE TRANSACTION

CHAPTER 5:
FORECLOSURES

CHAPTER 6:
MANUFACTURED HOUSING

CHAPTER 7:
HOUSING DISCRIMINATION

APPENDICES

ABOUT THE AUTHOR

MARGARET C. JASPER is an attorney engaged in the general practice of law in South Salem, New York, concentrating in the areas of personal injury and entertainment law. Ms. Jasper holds a Juris Doctor degree from Pace University School of Law, White Plains, New York, is a member of the New York and Connecticut bars, and is certified to practice before the United States District Courts for the Southern and Eastern Districts of New York, and the United States Supreme Court. Ms. Jasper has been appointed to the panel of arbitrators of the American Arbitration Association and the law guardian panel for the Family Court of the State of New York, is a member of the Association of Trial Lawyers of America, and is a New York State licensed real estate broker and member of the Westchester County Board of Realtors, operating as Jasper Real Estate, in South Salem, New York.

Ms. Jasper is the author and general editor of the following legal almanacs: Juvenile Justice and Children's Law; Marriage and Divorce; Estate Planning; The Law of Contracts; The Law of Dispute Resolution; Law for the Small Business Owner; The Law of Personal Injury; Real Estate Law for the Homeowner and Broker; Everyday Legal Forms; Dictionary of Selected Legal Terms; The Law of Medical Malpractice; The Law of Product Liability; The Law of No-Fault Insurance; The Law of Immigration; The Law of Libel and Slander; The Law of Buying and Selling; Elder Law; The Right to Die; AIDS Law; The Law of Obscenity and Pornography; The Law of Child Custody; The Law of Debt Collection; Consumer Rights Law; Bankruptcy Law for the Individual Debtor; Victim's Rights Law; Animal Rights Law; Workers' Compensation Law; Employee Rights in the Workplace; Probate Law; Environmental Law; Labor Law; The Americans with Disabilities Act; The Law of Capital Punishment; Education Law; The Law of Violence Against Women; Landlord-Tenant Law; Insurance Law; Religion and the Law; Commercial Law; Motor Vehicle Law; Social Security Law; The Law of Drunk Driving; The Law of Speech and the First Amendment; Employment Discrimination Under Title VII; Hospital Liability Law; Home Mortgage Law Primer; Copyright Law; Patent Law; Trademark Law; and Special Education Law.

INTRODUCTION

Owning one's home is the American dream. Home ownership carries with it a multitude of benefits generally not available to those who lease or rent. For example, owning a home is often less expensive than renting property, and ownership affords tax deductions which are not available to the renter. There is also long-term security and flexibility in home ownership whereas a renter is subject to the landlord's requirements. In addition, the value of property generally increases even as the value of paper money decreases.

This trend towards home ownership is also due, in large part, to a change in demographics, i.e., a growth in single person and lower income households, which cannot afford the ever increasing costs of rental. In addition, rent control discourages investment in rental housing because it limits the rents that the landlord can charge, leading to deterioration of the housing due to lack of sufficient funds for proper upkeep of the property. Thus, many rental properties have been converted into cooperatives and condominiums.

This legal almanac explores the law of real estate and discusses the relationship between the real estate broker and the prospective buyer or seller of real property. This almanac also examines the historical development of real estate ownership; the current sources of real estate law; modern day real estate ownership and interests, the sale and transfer of real estate, basic real estate financing, housing discrimination, and the role of the real estate broker in the real estate transaction.

Insofar as this almanac sets forth a broad discussion of the general aspects of real estate law as it applies in most jurisdictions, the reader is advised to check the law of their own jurisdiction when researching a specific issue.

The Appendix provides resource directories, statutes and other pertinent information and data. The Glossary contains definitions of many of the terms used throughout the almanac.

CHAPTER 1:
OVERVIEW OF REAL PROPERTY LAW

HISTORICAL BACKGROUND

The English System

The English system of land ownership preceded the American system, and was vehemently rejected by the colonies. The English system, had its roots in feudalism. Under the feudal system, the king owned all of the real property, and he divided the property into parcels known as feuds, which were given out to lords who were in service to the king. The lords would then grant a sublease to their own subjects. This is the origin of the word "landlord."

The lords did not enjoy outright ownership. Their rights were always conditioned upon their continued service to the monarchy. This system, known as feudal tenure, is similar to our current system of real estate leasing. The lords only enjoyed the right to the land during their lifetime. This changed in the late thirteenth century, when the lords were given the right to pass their interest in the land on to their heirs. As time passed, more and more rights in the land were surrendered by the monarchy.

The American Colonies

Although the feudal system had drastically changed by the time of the American Revolution, there remained a restrictive nature on land ownership in England. The colonists were pursuing the dream of absolute ownership of their piece of the new world. This restrictiveness was not acceptable to them, and was a major cause of the colonial revolt.

This led to the form of land ownership in the United States known as the allodial system. Under the allodial system, the titled owner of the property owns it absolutely, subject to the restrictions set forth by the established laws and regulations which govern real estate ownership in America.

THE SOURCES OF REAL ESTATE LAW

The law of real estate is derived from numerous sources, the most important of which is the United States Constitution. All other laws and regulations, whether they are enacted by a state or local government, by a judicial ruling, or privately between landowners, must not conflict with the rights guaranteed by the Constitution.

Those constitutionally guaranteed rights include the Fifth Amendment which prohibits the federal government from depriving a person of their property without due process of law. The Fifth Amendment also prohibits the government from taking a person's private property for public use without affording the property owner just compensation—known as the doctrine of eminent domain—discussed further below.

The Fourteenth Amendment provides the property owner with due process rights against state action, and further provides that all persons are to be given equal protection under the laws, and equal opportunity for the ownership of land.

Other sources of real estate law include federal legislation; state constitutions and legislation; the laws of the local jurisdiction in which the property is located, such as the county or town; and the law which is handed down by judicial rulings to clarify the broader existing law when a dispute arises. Of course, individual landowners are also permitted to create regulations, for example, in providing contractual obligations in the sale of real estate, and in placing covenants, easements and other restrictions in the deed transferring the property.

REAL ESTATE INTERESTS

The terms "real estate" and "real property" are often used interchangeably, however, there is a difference. Real estate refers to the land and its fixtures. The fixtures are items which are permanently attached to the land—such as the windows and doors—and are no longer considered personal property separate and apart from the land. Real property refers to the real estate and all of the rights of ownership to the real estate.

Interests in Land

The ownership of land is defined by the quality and extent of the interest that the owner has in the property. Such land interests are classified as (1) freehold estates; and (2) non-freehold estates.

Freehold Estate

A freehold estate is an interest in real property which has no measurable length of time and no termination date. Freehold estates include:

Fee Simple Absolute

Fee simple absolute refers to the most complete form of ownership of property, subject only to the restrictions discussed below.

Life Estate

A life estate is an ownership interest in the property for one's lifetime, or as measured by the lifetime of a third party. For example, A may grant B an interest in A's property for the rest of B's life. After B dies, A's property goes back to A, or to A's heirs should A have died. A may choose to use another person's life—such as C—as the measuring stick for the time B may have the property. Thus, when C dies, B must convey the property back to A or A's heirs.

Nonfreehold Estate

A nonfreehold estate, also known as a leasehold estate, is an interest in property which is fixed for a certain period of time, i.e., a tenancy of some type. Nonfreehold estates include:

Estate For Years

An estate for years is what is commonly known as a rental. The landlord gives the tenant a lease for a certain term during which the tenant is obligated to pay the landlord rent.

Estate From Period to Period

An estate from period to period, such as a month to month tenancy, is a rental which does not have a specifically stated duration, but which is terminated when either the landlord or the tenant gives due notice to the other party.

Estate At Will

An estate at will is similar to the estate from period to period, however, it is terminable at the will of either party. Some jurisdictions, however, have enacted legislation requiring that the landlord give the tenant notice a certain period of time before the termination takes effect.

Estate By Sufferance

An estate by sufferance refers to a tenant who comes into possession of the property lawfully, but who remains in possession after his or her legal right to the property has expired. For example, if at the end of a 1-year lease, the landlord and tenant have not signed a new lease, and the tenant remains in possession of the property, the interest becomes like an estate at will, which is terminable by either party until a new lease is signed.

Other Interests In Land

Adverse Possession

Adverse possession refers to the acquisition of land over the rights of all other persons, including the recorded landowner, by one who has openly, exclusively and continuously possessed the land for a statutory period of time, e.g., a period of 10 years. If the record owner, or other interested person, does not come forward within the required time period, title to the property goes to the possessor of the land.

Acquisition of land by adverse possession may occur when there has been an encroachment upon neighboring land. For example, John Doe builds a fence around his property approximately two feet beyond his property line into Mary Smith's land. It is an open and obvious encroachment upon her land. If this fence is permitted to remain upon the land for the statutory period of time, John Doe may be able to claim title to the encroached property under the doctrine of adverse possession.

License

License is a nonpossessory interest in property whereby the right is given to another to enter one's land for a specific purpose, e.g., to mine ore. The right may be revoked at any time by the landowner, unless a fee has been paid for that right, in which case the licensee has a contractual right for whatever duration to use the land for the purpose specified in the license.

Liens

Liens are interests in property which have a potential of being possessory. If the lien is not satisfied, the holder of the lien may proceed to sell or take possession of the property. Types of liens include mortgage liens, which are given to the lender in order to secure repayment of the mortgage note; and mechanic's liens, which are given to persons who furnish labor or materials for the improvement of the property.

Restrictions on Absolute Ownership

Although the allodial system of real estate purports to give the owner outright and absolute title to the property, in reality, those rights do have some significant restrictions, as further discussed below.

Property Taxes

The assessment of taxes upon a property owner is a form of restriction on the absolute ownership of property, which carries with it some justification. Property owners benefit from a wide variety of services which are provided by their local government, such as schools and libraries, law enforcement, and other municipal services. It costs money to operate all of these services, and the local government relies on taxes assessed on the property owners to help foot the bill.

However, because it would be unfair to tax all property owners equally, regardless of the size of land they own, each piece of property is individually assessed for value, and the tax is based on that assessment, known as an ad valorem real estate tax. The assessments are periodically reevaluated, e.g., every ten years. If a property owner fails to pay the property tax, the taxing authority has the right to seize and sell the property to recover the unpaid taxes.

Eminent Domain

Eminent domain refers to the power of the government, by specific legislation, to take private property if it serves a public interest. This is also known as condemnation. The governmental body which takes the property is required to give the owner and all other interest parties notice and a right to be heard. The government is further required to pay the owner the fair market value for the property.

The government is also entitled to delegate this power to other organizations, such as utility companies, if the property is necessary to the development of services. However, utilities often seek an easement on the property, rather than an outright takeover of the property. An easement is a nonpossessory interest in the land which permits the holder of the easement to use the land. For example, a utility company may run power lines underneath the property.

Zoning

Zoning refers to the approved use of a particular piece of property. For example, a developer who owns a 20-acre piece of land may desire to build 20 single family residences, each on a one-acre lot. However, the local zoning board may have established a two-acre lot minimum per residence. Obviously, this has a tremendous impact on the economic value of the property. The developer may apply for a variance—permission to "vary" from the existing zoning ordinance. If approved, the developer is permitted to go forward with the building plans even though they do not conform to the existing zoning laws. In general, properties which do not conform to the zoning law because they predated the legislation are not considered in violation of the law.

Escheat

Escheat refers to the law of some jurisdictions which holds that the title to property owned by a person who dies without a will, and without heirs, may revert—or "escheat"—to the state.

FORMS OF OWNERSHIP

Ownership in property refers to the holding of rights or interest in real estate. As set forth below, real estate may be owed in severalty, or jointly.

Ownership in Severalty

Ownership in severalty merely refers to sole ownership of real estate. The owner may be an individual, a corporation, a trust or any other entity, who owns the real estate outright without any co-owners.

Co-Ownership

Co-ownership refers to the holding of the rights and interest in real estate by two or more individuals or entities. There are several forms of co-ownership of real estate, including:

Joint Tenancy

A joint tenancy is created when an equal interest in the real estate is acquired simultaneously by two or more joint tenants, with the intent of forming a joint tenancy, each being given the same degree of ownership and the same right to possess the whole property.

Joint tenancy creates a right of survivorship, which means that upon the death of any of the joint tenants, that tenant's interest does not pass by will or inheritance, but the entire interest in the property passes to the surviving tenant(s). If there is any question about the intent to create a joint tenancy, then the tenancy may be deemed a tenancy in common.

If a joint tenant no longer wishes to own the property jointly, the joint tenant can apply to the court to partition the property amongst the joint owners, thus creating a tenancy in common. Creditors of one joint tenant can also proceed against a joint tenant to satisfy a debt, thus partitioning the property. The creditor then becomes a tenant in common with the remaining tenants.

Tenancy in Common

Tenancy in common is how most property is held between two or more individuals who do not expressly intend to hold the property as joint tenants.

Tenants in common each own an undivided interest in the property, as well as an undivided right to possess the whole property. They each have the right to sell or mortgage their interest in the property. Upon the death of a tenant in common, their interest passes to their heirs.

Tenancy by the Entirety

Tenancy by the entirety is generally the form of ownership taken by, and available only to, a husband and wife, absent an express provision that the property is being held as a joint tenancy or a tenancy in common. Like a joint tenancy, tenants by the entirety each enjoy a right to survivorship. If the husband and wife divorce, their ownership in the property becomes a tenancy in common.

Other Common Forms of Ownership

Condominium Ownership

The condominium is a statutorily created form of ownership of real estate whereby each individual owns his or her own unit in fee simple, which may be mortgaged, and for which the owner pays property taxes. Each individual also owns an undivided interest in the common areas of the real estate, such as the hallways, recreational facilities, etc, for which they pay a common charge for the maintenance of those areas.

Each individual is entitled to vote on matters of interest based upon their ownership percentage of the common areas of the condominium. The by-laws of the condominium contain the rules and regulations of the condominium, and are part of the documents, including the declaration and plans of the condominium, which are required to be recorded with the county where the development is located.

Cooperative Ownership

Cooperative ownership, unlike the condominium, refers to the ownership of an entire multi-unit development by the tenants as a whole. Each tenant owns stock in the cooperative, which is usually a corporation. The corporation owns the real estate. Each tenant possesses his or her unit pursuant to a lease agreement with the corporation. There may be restrictions upon the sale of one's unit in that prior approval from the corporation is usually required.

Instead of rent, the cooperative owner pays what is known as maintenance, which usually includes the real estate taxes, the cost of maintaining the property, and a monthly assessment. The cooperative owner may also have taken out a loan for the purchase of the property, which is secured by his or her cooperative stock.

CHAPTER 2:
THE ROLE OF THE REAL ESTATE BROKER

IN GENERAL

The role of a real estate broker is varied, however, most people generally define a real estate broker as the person who is hired to assist in the sale or lease of property, by bringing together the seller and a qualified buyer. The real estate broker is an agent who acts on behalf of one or both of the parties to the transaction.

For the purposes of this section, the term broker and agent are used interchangeably. However, it should be noted, as is more fully explained later in this chapter, that a broker is an agent, but an agent—that is, a salesperson—may not necessarily be a broker, but may work under a broker's supervision.

The Seller's Agent

A seller's agent, also referred to as a listing agent, is employed by and represents only the seller in a transaction. The seller's agent is compensated by the seller, usually on a commission basis based on the selling price. The seller's agent is obligated to act in the seller's best interest. For example, the seller's agent must protect confidential information which may negatively impact the seller's bargaining position, such as a seller whose property is close to being foreclosed upon. The seller's agent is generally responsible for:

(1) Listing the property for sale, and placing it with a multiple listing service;

(2) Advertising the property;

(3) Negotiating the best price and terms for the sale of the property, and evaluating all offers.

The Subagent

The subagent also works for the seller, and splits the commission for the sale with the seller's agent, although a subagent is usually first contacted by the potential buyer. Nevertheless, in negotiating the purchase, the subagent represents the seller's best interests.

The Buyer's Agent

A buyer's agent is employed by and represents only the buyer. A buyer's agent may be compensated by the buyer, however, it is more typical that the buyer's agent, like a subagent, splits the commission with the seller's agent. The buyer's agent represents the buyer's best interests during all phases of the transaction.

The Dual Agent

A broker may act on behalf of both the seller and buyer. This is known as dual agency. Because it is important for the parties to know who the broker represents in the transaction, agency disclosure forms are generally prepared and signed by the parties. The disclosure forms explain the role of the broker and to whom the broker is bound to represent. This is particularly important in the case of a dual agency due to the appearance of a conflict of interest in the representation of both parties to the transaction.

A dual agent's objective is to sell the property, however, the dual agent does not give undivided loyalty to either party. Dual agency may occur even if the buyer is working with a different agent, if both agents are employed by the same brokerage office.

A sample agency disclosure and acknowledgment form is set forth at Appendix 1.

LICENSING REQUIREMENTS

All jurisdictions statutorily require that real estate brokers and salespersons obtain a license, to demonstrate that the broker or salesperson has met the jurisdiction's competency requirements. The licensing requirements are usually established by an administrative agency created by the state for that purpose.

The Model Licensing Requirements of the National Association of Real Estate License Law Officials (NARELLO) is set forth at Appendix 2.

A real estate salesperson is generally defined as one who performs any act specified in the definition of a real estate broker, but who does so under the direction, control or management of a broker. The possession of a real estate salesperson license for a minimum period of time is usually a prerequisite to obtaining a broker's license, and there is generally some type of continuing education requirement. The real estate broker is licensed to operate his or her own real estate brokerage office, unlike the real estate salesperson who must be sponsored by the broker in order to practice. The salesperson is generally hired as an independent contractor rather than an employee of the broker.

A sample broker/salesperson independent contractor agreement is set forth at Appendix 3.

Engaging in the Business of Real Estate

Engaging in the business of real estate without a valid salesperson or broker license is illegal, and an unlicenced person is prohibited from collecting a commission. Thus, it should be understood which activities are classified as "engaging in the business of real estate" so one knows what he or she is prohibited from doing without a license.

The Suggested Pattern Real Estate License Law of the National Association of Realtors sets forth a list of activities which would be considered acting in the capacity of a real estate broker, including:

(1) Selling, exchanging, purchasing, renting or leasing real estate;

(2) Offering to sell, exchange, purchase, rent or lease real estate;

(3) Negotiating, or offering, attempting or agreeing to negotiate the sale, exchange, purchase, rental or leasing of real estate;

(4) Listing, or offering, attempting or agreeing to list, real estate for sale, lease or exchange.

(5) Auctioning, or offering, attempting or agreeing to auction real estate;

(6) Buying, selling, or offering to buy or sell, or otherwise dealing in options on real estate or the improvements thereon;

(7) Collecting, or offering, attempting or agreeing to collect rent for the use of real estate;

(8) Advertising or holding oneself out as being engaged in the business of buying, selling, exchanging, renting or leasing real estate;

(9) Assisting or directing in the procurement of prospects calculated to result in the sale, exchange, lease or rental of real estate;

(10) Assisting or directing in the negotiation of any transaction calculated or intended to result in the sale, exchange, leasing or rental of real estate.

(11) Engaging in the business of charging an advance fee in connection with any contract whereby he or she undertakes to promote the sale or lease of real estate, either through its listing in a publication is-

sued for such purpose or for referral of information concerning such real estate to brokers, or both.

(12) Assisting or directing in the procurement or arrangement of mortgage financing on real property, or in obtaining a mortgagee or his agent who is authorized to make real property loans under state or federal authority and supervision, if the person is not acting in the capacity of a licensed mortgagee or his agent; and

(13) Performing any of the foregoing acts as an employee of, or on behalf of, the owner of real estate, or the owner of any interest therein, or the improvements affixed thereon, for compensation.

There are some jurisdictions which also include appraising and managing real property, and other activities closely related to property and land sales, as acting in the capacity of a real estate broker.

In some jurisdictions, the roles of real estate broker and real estate attorney overlap. It is generally held that a real estate broker may not prepare the documents necessary to close the real estate transaction, such as the sales contract, deed, lease, or any other instruments which are designed to create legal rights or impose legal responsibilities on third parties. However, a minority of jurisdictions now permit real estate brokers to prepare the legal documents which heretofore were solely prepared by the real estate attorney.

Persons Exempt from Licensing Requirement

As set forth in The Suggested Pattern Real Estate License Law of the National Association of Realtors®, certain individuals are exempt from the licensing requirement, as follows:

(1) The owner or lessor of the property concerned;

(2) An attorney-in-fact of the owner or lessor of the property concerned who is operating under a duly executed power of attorney;

(3) An attorney-at-law;

(4) A receiver, trustee in bankruptcy, executor or guardian;

(5) A resident manager;

(6) A federal, state or other governmental officer performing official duties; and

(7) Multiple listing services.

There are some jurisdictions which have granted additional exemptions from licensure which are not explicitly provided for in the above NAR list, including exemptions for banks and trust companies; auctioneers; sellers of cemetery lots, public utilities and railroads; and the clerical and non-sales employees of real estate brokers.

THE NATIONAL ASSOCIATION OF REALTORS®

The National Association of Realtors® (NAR) is the largest professional real estate organization. Membership in NAR is not mandatory for the practice of real estate. However, only members of NAR are permitted to use the designation "Realtor"®, which is NAR's registered trademark. NAR disseminates industry information to its members, provides educational opportunities for its membership, and sets forth a code of ethics to which the Realtor® members are deemed to have subscribed. The NAR also offers certification to members who have attained a certain level of competency in a particular designation.

There are many other organizations in the real estate industry which are designed to assist the membership in providing continuing education in the particular field.

A directory of the major real estate associations and their functions is set forth at Appendix 4.

PROPERTY LISTINGS

When a seller selects a certain broker to sell his or her property, the property is known as the broker's listing. An agreement, known as a listing agreement, is entered into between the broker and seller for a specified period of time. The listing agreement is a contract which specifically describes the property to be sold, and sets forth the rights, duties and responsibilities of the parties to the contract. The listing agreement is signed by both the broker and the seller.

There are several types of listing agreements depending on the rights being given to the broker, as set forth below.

Exclusive Agency Agreement

The exclusive agency agreement gives the listing broker the right to act as the seller's agent in the sale of the property, and to receive a commission if the broker finds a buyer. However, the seller retains the right to sell his or her own property without incurring a commission to the listing broker. Nevertheless, if the seller uses another broker to sell the property, other than the listing agent, the seller will be obligated to pay a commission to the original listing agent under the exclusive agency agreement, and an additional commission to the broker who actually sold the property.

A sample exclusive agency agreement is set forth at Appendix 5.

Exclusive Right To Sell Agreement

The exclusive right to sell agreement provides that the listing broker retains the right to receive a commission upon the sale of the property regardless of who is actually responsible for finding the buyer. The right to receive a commission applies even if the seller finds a buyer independent of the broker. This is obviously the most advantageous type of listing agreement for the broker.

A sample exclusive right to sell agreement is set forth at Appendix 6.

Open Listing

An open listing is one where the seller lists the property with more than one broker. The broker who actually sells the property is the only one entitled to the commission. If the seller is able to find a buyer without the assistance of a broker, the seller is not obligated to pay a commission.

THE MULTIPLE LISTING SERVICE

The multiple listing service (MLS) provides, on a regular basis, access to the listings of all brokers who are MLS members. This permits MLS members to show the listings of other broker members. If a buyer is obtained in this manner, the broker who found the buyer shares in the commission with the listing broker according to a prearranged fee splitting provision.

OBLIGATIONS

A broker has certain responsibilities to the parties involved in the real estate transaction, as set forth below.

Broker's Obligations to the Seller

Because the listing agreement establishes the broker as the agent of the seller, the common-law principles of agency law apply. The broker has an ongoing fiduciary responsibility to act in the best interests of the seller during all phases of the real estate transaction. The broker has a duty of care to make sure that the property is properly marketed, and that the details, advantages and disadvantages of all offers are fully explained to the seller. The broker also has a duty of loyalty to the seller, and cannot be compensated by any other party to the transaction unless there has been full disclosure and an agreement to the dual agency representation.

The scope of the broker's authority to act is set forth in the listing agreement, and the broker is liable to the seller if the broker in any way exceeds the extent of this authority. For example, if the seller wants the property listed for $200,000, the broker cannot unilaterally accept an offer of less than the stated amount without first consulting with the seller. If so, the broker may be held liable to the seller for the difference between the list price and the accepted offer.

Broker's Obligations to the Buyer

If the broker is a buyer's broker, then the same agency principles of duty and loyalty discussed above apply to their relationship. In that situation, the broker has a fiduciary responsibility to the buyer to act in the buyer's best interests. The broker's role in that relationship is to find a property for the buyer that meets all of the criteria set forth by the buyer.

Further, even though the broker usually has no contractual relationship with the buyer, he or she may still be liable to the buyer if the broker makes any misrepresentations—either intentionally or negligently—about the property being sold. Forms of misrepresentation include:

(1) The intentional nondisclosure of the condition of the property and any known defects;

(2) Advising the buyer that there are other offers, when in fact there are none, in an effort to force the buyer to act quickly; and

(3) negligently stating facts about the property without making a sufficient investigation into the actual facts.

Broker's Obligations to Other Real Estate Professionals

The broker who hires salespersons to work in the brokerage office has certain responsibilities to those salespersons. A salesperson is usually deemed an independent contractor. An agreement which clearly explains that role, and the rights and obligations of the broker-salesperson relationship, as well as the rights and responsibilities among the office's salespersons, should be executed. In particular, the fee splitting arrangement between the broker and the salesperson should be clearly explained.

The broker also has a responsibility to deal fairly with other brokers, particularly in determining entitlement to real estate commissions, and in non-interference with existing contractual relationships between brokers and their clients.

Broker's Obligation to the State

A broker is at risk of having their licensed revoked if they do not adhere to certain state laws and regulations governing the practice of real estate. Some of the most common statutory violations applicable to the majority of jurisdictions include:

(1) The unauthorized practice of law, when a broker exceeds the authority granted;

(2) Fee splitting with unlicensed individuals;

(3) Commingling client funds with broker funds; and

(4) Misrepresentation in advertising;

(5) Discriminatory practices, such as refusing to show properties on the basis of race, national origin or sex. A discussion of housing discrimination is set forth in Chapter 7 of this almanac.

BROKER COMPENSATION

Broker compensation is usually stated as a percentage of the sale price of the property, e.g. six percent. In general, the broker is entitled to the commission when the broker produces a buyer who is ready, willing and able to purchase the property according to the terms of the listing agreement. A buyer is deemed "ready and willing" when they express an interest in purchasing the property according to the terms set forth by the seller, and make payments which evidence their intention. A buyer is considered "able" when it is determined that they either have the necessary funds, or qualify for sufficient financing, to purchase the property.

The right to a commission upon producing a buyer who is "ready, willing and able," protects the broker should the seller try to back out of the deal, or try to negotiate directly with the prospective buyer. Thus, in the majority of jurisdictions, the broker's commission is not contingent upon the actual closing of the real estate transaction. Nevertheless, most commissions are actually paid to the broker, at the closing, from the proceeds of the sale.

CHAPTER 3:
BUYING AND SELLING REAL ESTATE

BUYING A HOME

The Advantages of Home Ownership

One of the biggest decisions an individual may make in their life is whether to rent their living quarters or to buy a home. Aside from the peace of mind you gain knowing that you are solely in charge of your living space, there are a number of additional factors which make owning a home more attractive then renting.

The value of your real property is likely to increase over the years whereas if you rent you do not benefit at all in any increase in property value. If you obtain a mortgage, the interest is tax deductible and, during the first half of the loan period, the majority of the monthly payment is all interest. The homeowner may also deduct property taxes.

Costs

One obstacle an individual faces when buying a home is coming up with enough money to complete the transaction. The amount of money needed to buy a home depends on a number of factors, including the cost of the house and the type of mortgage obtained. In general, the prospective home buyer may need the following funds:

Earnest Money

Earnest money is the initial deposit made on a home when the offer is submitted. The earnest money deposit demonstrates to the seller that you are serious about purchasing the home. If the offer is accepted, the real estate broker or the seller's attorney generally deposits the earnest money in an escrow account until closing. At closing, the escrowed funds are used to offset the downpayment or other closing costs. If the offer is not accepted, the earnest money is refunded.

The Down Payment

The down payment is a percentage of the cost of the home that you must pay at closing. An average down payment is twenty (20%) percent of the purchase price of the home. The higher the down payment, the lower the monthly mortgage payments will be. Some government mortgages, such as FHA mortgages, only require a three (3%) percent down payment.

Closing Costs

As further discussed in Chapter 4, the closing costs are the costs associated with processing the paperwork necessary to purchase the home, and the various fees your lender charges. The law requires that the lender provide the mortgage applicant an estimate of the closing costs.

Finding a Lender

A mortgage loan may be obtained from a bank, a savings and loan, a credit union, a private mortgage company, or from various state government lenders. Different lenders can offer quite different interest rates and loan fees so it is wise to shop around. The lower the interest, the smaller the monthly payment. Prior to shopping around for a home, it is advisable to visit a lender to find out what price range you should be considering in purchasing your home.

Pre-Qualification

A lender will generally "pre-qualify" a borrower based on some basic information provided over the phone, such as income, debt, and the amount of down-payment available. The lender will then tell the borrower the amount of loan he may be able to obtain. The lender generally does not require verification of the information given at this point and is not obligated to fund the loan. However, this process gives the prospective homeowner an idea of the price range of houses he or she should consider.

Pre-Approval

Pre-approval is the lender's actual commitment to make the loan. It involves assembling the financial records and going through a preliminary approval process. Pre-approval gives the prospective buyer a definite idea of what he or she can afford and demonstrates that the buyer is serious about purchasing a home.

In deciding whether to approve a loan, the lender considers the loan applicant's debt-to-income ratio, i.e., a comparison of the gross income before taxes to the housing and non-housing expenses. Non-housing expenses include such long-term debts as car or student loan payments, alimony, and/or child support.

According to the Federal Housing Administration (FHA), monthly mortgage payments should be no more than 29% of gross income, while the mortgage payment, combined with non-housing expenses, should total no more than 41% of income. The lender also considers cash available for down payment and closing costs, credit history, etc. when determining the maximum loan amount.

A lender will generally ask the prospective applicant to provide the following documentation:

- Pay stubs for the past 2-3 months
- W-2 forms for the past 2 years
- Information on long-term debts
- Recent bank statements
- Tax returns for the past 2 years
- Proof of any other income
- Address and description of the property you wish to buy
- Sales contract

The lender will also order the applicant's credit report and will conduct an appraisal of the property to make sure it meets the lender's loan to value requirement.

Within three days of making a loan application, the lender is required to supply the applicant with a good faith estimate of all fees paid before closing, all closing costs, and any escrow costs they will encounter when purchasing a home. It takes approximately 3-6 weeks to obtain approval for a loan.

It is important that the prospective home buyer has a steady source of reliable income and is not overwhelmed with debt which would make the mortgage payment too burdensome to manage. The homeowner must pay the mortgage payment on time each month or risk losing their home.

For a complete discussion of the mortgage loan process, the reader is advised to consult this author's legal almanac entitled Home Mortgage Law Primer published by Oceana Publishing Company.

Finding a Real Estate Agent

As soon as you decide that you are going to buy a home, you should find an experienced real estate professional to assist you. You may be able to obtain referrals from friends or relatives who have worked with a particular agent, particularly in the area you are seeking to purchase your home. If you drive through the prospective neighborhood, many agents have their names listed on signs outside of the properties being sold.

As set forth in Chapter 2, there are real estate agents who represent buyers only, sellers only, and those who represent both buyers and sellers—dual agents. A seller's agent's fiduciary duty is to the seller. However, even though a seller's agent generally has no contractual relationship with the buyer, he or she may still be liable to the buyer if they make any misrepresentations—either intentionally or negligently—about the property being sold. Broker misrepresentation is more fully discussed in Chapter 2.

The dual agent works for both the buyer and seller with their consent. However, you must be aware that all agents are primarily concerned with making the sale so that they earn their commission.

If you deal with a buyer's agent, that agent's duty is to the buyer at all stages of the transaction. The agent's role in that relationship is to find a property for the buyer that meets all of the criteria set forth by the buyer. Typically, the buyer's agent, like a subagent, takes a percentage of the commission earned by the broker who lists the property. The prospective buyer generally does not pay anything for the services provided by the agent.

It is important to take the time to interview the agent to see if you are compatible because you will be spending a lot of time with him or her while you search for your ideal home, and will have to place a certain amount of trust in their knowledge and abilities. Make sure they are well advised about the type of house you are looking for and are aware of your requirements and desires.

Finding the Right Home

Before you begin viewing homes, it is helpful to establish a list of criteria you are looking for in a home. Sort out the essential qualities from the non-essential and don't waste time looking at houses that don't meet your minimum requirements.

Size

It is important to consider the size of the home one wishes to purchase. One must contemplate how much space is needed to comfortably accommodate the family. According to the United States Department of Housing and Urban Development (HUD), in assessing a prospective property, one should consider the following factors:

• Is there enough room for both the present and the future?

• Are there enough bedrooms and bathrooms?

• Is the house structurally sound?

• Do the mechanical systems and appliances work?

• Is the yard big enough?

• Do you like the floor plan?

• Will your furniture fit in the space?

• Is there enough storage space?

• Does anything need to repaired or replaced? If so, will the seller repair or replace the items?

• Imagine the house in good weather and bad, and in each season. Will you be happy with it all year round?

Location

It is also important to consider the location of the home and its proximity to work, school, transportation, shopping, etc. It is also a good idea to spend some time in the area to try and get a feel for the community. One can contact the local chamber of commerce for information. The local library can also be an excellent source for information on local events and resources.

Schools

If you have children or are planning a family, you should inquire about the schools in the district. You can get information about school systems by contacting the city or county school board or the local schools. Your real estate agent may also be knowledgeable about schools in the area. Take the time to visit the school if it is in session and speak with the administrators and the parents of other children who attend the school.

Home Inspection

It is prudent to have a qualified and experienced home inspector check the safety of the prospective home before you make a formal offer. Once you have closed the deal, you are generally stuck with the cost of any repairs that need to be made. If you are unable to conduct a home inspection before making the offer, you should include an inspection clause in the contract which requires the homeowner to undertake any necessary repairs that may be needed prior to closing. The inspection clause should also allow for a price readjustment if serious problems are found, and/or permit the prospective buyer to opt out of the sale.

Home inspectors focus on the structure, construction, and mechanical systems of the house. The home inspector reports on any necessary repairs. Generally, an inspector checks and gives repair estimates on the electrical system, plumbing and waste disposal, the water heater, insulation and ventilation, the HVAC system, water source and quality, the potential presence of pests, the foundation, doors, windows, ceilings, walls, floors, and roof.

If a problem is discovered that involves health-related risks, such as those involving asbestos, lead paint, water, or waste disposal problems, it is best to get a specialist in to assess the particular problem. If the home was built before 1978, and you have children under the age of seven, you should be aware that lead flakes from paint can be present in both the home and in the soil surrounding the house. The problem can be fixed temporarily by repairing damaged paint surfaces or planting grass over effected soil. However, hiring a lead abatement contractor to remove paint chips and seal damaged areas will fix the problem permanently.

Making an Offer

There are several factors to consider in making an offer on a home, such as whether the asking price is in line with comparable recent home sales; the condition of the home and cost of any necessary repairs; the length of time the house has been on the market; the seller's situation; whether there are other offers being made on the house; the mortgage amount you will be required to obtain; and whether you are really happy with the house. After you make your initial offer, the buyer will most likely counter-offer and offers and counter-offers will be exchanged until you can agree to a purchase price.

SELLING YOUR HOME

In General

Selling one's home can be an emotional time. There are often many memories connected with a home that people are reluctant to leave behind yet there is also the excitement of starting anew in another location. It is also at this most vulnerable time that the seller must remain level-headed and attentive to details connected with the sale of the home.

The chances are that you will be moving into a new home and the purchase of that new home is contingent upon the sale of the present home. Therefore, it is advisable to place the present home on the market well in advance of the new purchase. Otherwise, you may be in the position of having to close on the new home without the funds you expected to have from the sale of the former home, or you will be stuck with carrying the expenses of two homes at the same time until the first home sells.

Getting Your Home Ready

First impressions are generally the strongest. Thus, it is important to make sure that your home's exterior is in good condition. While the house is on the market, it is important to maintain the lawn and landscaping. If there are any visually offensive repairs which need to be made, it is advisable to do so. Putting a fresh coat of paint on doorways and window frames and shutters is generally an inexpensive way to enhance the appearance of the home.

Making sure the interior is clean is an extremely important factor in selling your home. Rugs and floors should be cleaned thoroughly. Remove unnecessary furniture and other items to make the rooms look as spacious as possible. Appliances should be meticulously scrubbed clean. Make cosmetic repairs, however, expensive home improvements—such as renovating the kitchen—are generally not necessary and may not be cost-effective. Flood the home with light—open windows and pull back draperies. A coat of paint on the walls will brighten up the home.

Listing the Property with a Broker

You must decide whether you want to try and sell your home or retain a real estate professional to handle all aspects of the listing, such as advertising the property, showing the property and conducting an "open house" for potential buyers. Obviously, if you sell your home yourself, you will save the commission—usually 6%—earned by the real estate agent upon the sale of the home. A discussion of For Sale By Owner listings is set forth below.

As further discussed in Chapter 2, a real estate agent generally performs valuable services for the seller. For example, they will list the property with a multiple listing service, i.e., a database used by all real estate agents who are searching for properties for potential buyers. This will give the home more exposure than if you merely list the property in local newspapers. The real estate agent also advertises the property and sets up appointments to show the home to potential buyers. The real estate agent also serves as the intermediary between you and the prospective buyer while negotiating for a mutually agreeable purchase price.

Prior to retaining a real estate agent to represent you, it is important to try and obtain recommendations and referrals. You should also get a written commitment from the agent on what services they will perform and how they plan to market your home.

When a seller selects a certain broker to sell his or her property, the property is known as the broker's listing. An agreement, known as a listing agreement, is entered into between the broker and seller for a specified period of time. Try and negotiate a mutually satisfactory commission prior to signing any listing agreement. You should also try and obtain a short term agreement—e.g. 90 days—with the real estate agent during which time you can judge whether he or she is doing a good job representing your interests.

The listing agreement is a contract which specifically describes the property to be sold, and sets forth the rights, duties and responsibilities of the parties to the contract. The listing agreement is signed by both the broker and the seller. As more fully discussed in Chapter 2, there are several types of listing agreements depending on the rights being given to the broker, as set forth below, including:

1. The Exclusive Agency agreement;

2. The Exclusive Right To Sell Agreement;

3. The Open Listing.

The scope of the broker's authority to act is set forth in the listing agreement, and the broker is liable to the seller if the broker in any way exceeds the extent of this authority. Because the listing agreement establishes the broker as the agent of the seller, the common-law principles of agency law apply. The broker has an ongoing fiduciary responsibility to act in the best interests of the seller during all phases of the real estate transaction.

The broker has a duty of care to make sure that the property is properly marketed, and that the details, advantages and disadvantages of all offers are fully explained to the seller. The broker also has a duty of loyalty to the seller, and cannot be compensated by any other party to the transaction unless there has been full disclosure and an agreement to the dual agency representation.

The List Price

Deciding upon a fair list price for your home is very important. Obviously, you want to get as high a price as possible for your home. The list price must fairly compensate you for the value of your home, but it should not be so inflated as to deter potential buyers who are shopping in a specific price range. If you must later drastically reduce the list price to attract buyers, they may wonder whether a problem with the home caused you to drop the price.

The real estate agent will be able to assist you in setting a fair list price for your home, taking into account such variables as the location and condition of the home, the housing market condition, comparable sales, and extra features your home may include, such as an in-ground pool, finished basement, etc.

The broker cannot unilaterally accept an offer of less than the established list price without first consulting with the seller. If so, the broker may be held liable to the seller for the difference between the list price and the accepted offer.

For Sale By Owner Listing

For Sale by Owner listings make up approximately one-fifth of all real estate sales in the United States. Although a seller may be able to save a considerate amount in commissions by selling their home on their own, it can be costly and quite difficult to market a property, particularly when sales are slow.

Discount brokerage services have entered this "for sale by owner" market to try and give sellers more marketing options at a reduced rate than a full-service listing agreement with a traditional real estate agency. Typically, a discount broker will charge a flat fee or reduced commission for the services they provide. However, it is important to know what services the discount broker intends to provide in exchange for their fee, and to have that agreement set forth in writing.

One advantage to using a discount broker is that they generally will be able to have your property listed with the local multiple listing service (MLS). This will give your property the greatest exposure. However, in order to have your property listed with the MLS, the seller must generally agree to pay a co-brokerage fee to any agent who provides a buyer for the property. Typically, you will have to pay approximately one-half of what the commission would be if you list the property with a full-service broker.

Screening Prospective Buyers

It is important to set some type of guidelines for screening prospective buyers so that valuable time is not wasted on those who cannot qualify for a loan or otherwise afford to purchase your home. This is particularly important if you plan to take your home off the market upon acceptance of an offer. As stated above, a buyer may be pre-qualified for a certain loan amount but that does not guarantee that the lender will fund the loan whereas a buyer who is pre-approved should be able to close the transaction.

Prior to accepting an offer, the agent—or the seller if he or she is marketing the home without an agent—will generally want to obtain the buyer's credit report, income and employment information, and find out whether the sale is contingent on the buyer selling another property, the source of the buyer's downpayment and financing, and the time the buyer will need to close the real estate transaction.

Legal Representation

It is advisable to seek legal representation when selling your home, particularly if you plan to sell the home without retaining a real estate professional. You should retain an attorney who specializes in the area of real estate law. Your attorney will prepare any legal documents you need, including the real estate sales contract. Your attorney will make sure that the buyer complies timely with all the contingencies so that the sale is not unduly delayed. Your attorney will represent you at the closing and make sure all of the legal documents are correct.

Tax Consequences

It is important to consult a tax professional when planning to sell your home. The sale of a home can have major federal and state tax implications, such as capital gain taxes, i.e., taxes which may be assessed on any gain from the sale of the home. Generally, if you purchase another home of equal or greater value within two years after selling your home the capital gain tax may be deferred.

CHAPTER 4:
THE REAL ESTATE TRANSACTION

LEGAL REPRESENTATION

Some states require a lawyer to assist in several aspects of the home buying process while other states do not, as long as a qualified real estate professional is involved. However, even if your state doesn't require one, you may want to hire a lawyer to help with the complex paperwork and legal contracts. A lawyer can review contracts, make you aware of special considerations, and assist you with the closing process.

THE PRE-CONTRACT STAGE

The pre-contract stage of the real estate transaction begins when the buyer makes an offer on the property, and the seller accepts the offer. Following acceptance of the offer, a memorandum of agreement is usually prepared. The memorandum sets forth the basic details of the transaction, and identifies the brokers, the parties, and their respective attorneys. In some jurisdictions, a binder—payment of a small sum of money which evidences the buyer's good faith—is made. This payment is also known as the earnest money deposit. The legal enforceability of the binder as a contract is questionable, thus, it should not be depended upon in order to secure the deal.

THE REAL ESTATE CONTRACT

The next step in the real estate transaction involves drafting the real estate contract, which is generally done by the seller's attorney. The contracts are then sent to the buyer's attorney for review and signature, and returned to the seller's attorney with the buyer's downpayment, which is held in escrow until closing.

Legal Requirements

The real estate contract, to be valid, must contain all of the essential terms of a legal contract, including an offer; acceptance of the offer; and consideration, i.e., an exchange of something of value by each of the parties. Further, the parties to the contract must be legally competent, must have voluntarily entered into the contract, and the contract must be for a legal purpose which is possible to perform.

The Statute of Frauds

The statute of frauds is a legal doctrine which provides, in part, that all contracts for the sale and purchase of real estate are required to be in writing. Further, the writing must be signed by the parties.

Purpose

Property can be legally conveyed without a real estate contract. However, the purpose of the contract is to create a legal obligation between the parties to perform as agreed. For example, without the contract, one of the parties could simply renege on the deal, and the other party would not have any legal recourse. The contract provides specific remedies in case one of the parties defaults, such as forfeiture of the downpayment to the seller, or money damages to the buyer.

Specific Performance

Because land is considered unique, and money damages may not be a sufficient remedy to the buyer, the doctrine of specific performance may apply. If the buyer sues for specific performance—i.e. to force the seller to perform under the contract—the judge may compel the seller to turn the property over to the buyer as agreed.

Financing Contingencies

The contract also sets forth the financing contingencies of the buyer, which basically permits the buyer to get out of the contract if he or she is unable to secure the type of financing set forth in the contract. For example, the contract may specify a mortgage contingency of 90% financing of the purchase price. If the buyer is unable to qualify for a loan on those terms, but the lender agrees to finance 80%, the buyer has the option of going forward with the lesser financing, or of invoking the mortgage contingency clause to get out of the contract without losing the downpayment. However, if the buyer qualifies for the 90% loan, he or she must go forward with the purchase, or risk forfeiting the downpayment to the seller for damages.

Physical Inspection

The contract may also provide remedies if a physical inspection of the property reveals any problems, such as termite infestation or structural damage. Such remedies may include a purchase price reduction, or a requirement that the necessary repairs be made as a condition to closing.

Title Search

It is also during the contract phase that the legal status of the property is researched to make sure that the seller can convey marketable title. This is known as a title search. The title search also reveals any liens or encumbrances that may exist against the property, which must be satisfied at or before closing. This search is undertaken by a title company hired by the purchaser to research the title. The buyer also may purchase title insurance from the title company, as is further discussed below under closing costs.

REAL ESTATE FINANCING

A buyer may purchase the property on an all cash basis, in which case the parties would basically go straight to closing. However, it is more likely that the buyer will be obtaining a large part of the purchase price through a lender. The most common lenders are banks and mortgage companies. After the contracts are signed, they are usually sent to the buyer's lender for review—the last major step before closing.

Mortgages and Lender's Rights

A mortgage represents the lender's security interest in the real estate. The mortgage remains as a lien on the property until the underlying debt is paid in full. If the borrower defaults on the mortgage payments, the lender has the right to foreclose on the property and sell it. The proceeds of the foreclosure sale are applied against the debt. If there is still an amount owing after the sale, the lender has the right to seek a deficiency judgment against the borrower for the additional amount owed. Alternatively, if the sale yields a profit, any amounts received above the outstanding debt are returned to the borrower.

The fact that the lender has a security interest in the property does not preclude the owner from selling the property. Nevertheless, the debt must be satisfied as a condition of the sale. This usually occurs at the closing. The proceeds of the sale are used to satisfy the debt.

If the property were to be sold without the debt being satisfied, then the buyer would be accepting the property "subject to" the existing mortgage. This means that the lender retains its security interest in the property even though there is a different owner. The seller also remains personally liable for payment of the debt. Although the buyer is not personally liable for the debt because the buyer was not a party to the mortgage, the buyer can still lose the property in a foreclosure sale if the seller defaults on the mortgage payments.

Nevertheless, if the buyer expressly "assumes" the existing mortgage debt, the buyer also becomes liable for the debt. In this case, the lender may collect the outstanding debt from either the seller or the buyer. The seller is not relieved from its obligation under the mortgage unless the lender expressly agrees to substitute the buyer for the seller. However, this lessens the lender's remedies should there be a default.

Legal Requirements

Like a contract, a mortgage has certain requirements which must be satisfied in order for it to be valid. The mortgage must be in writing and signed by all of the parties who have an interest in the property. The parties must have their signatures acknowledged before a notary public. Further the parties must be competent and of legal age to enter into the mortgage.

First Mortgage

The lender usually retains a first mortgage on the property, which generally gives the lender the first right to the property if the borrower defaults. Mortgages made after the first mortgage are considered subordinate mortgages. The holder of a subordinate mortgage must wait until the first mortgagee is paid before recovering the debt owed on the subordinate mortgage. This is a precarious position to be in because if the sale does not result in enough money to cover both mortgages, the subordinate mortgagee is not paid in full, if at all. Nevertheless, the subordinate mortgagee still retains the right to go directly after the borrower for any deficiencies in recovery.

Amortized Mortgage

The most common mortgage utilized is the amortized mortgage. The amortized mortgage provides for a set monthly payment plan over a stated term, e.g., 30 years. Each monthly payment consists of both principal and interest. In the early years of the loan, the interest is usually the larger share of the payment. As the loan term comes to a close, the principal payment makes up the larger share of the payment. At the end of the loan period, the entire principal and interest debt is repaid.

A mortgage payment estimation chart is set forth at Appendix 7.

Adjustable Rate Mortgage

Adjustable rate mortgages are also commonly used. An adjustable rate mortgage does not have a fixed payment, but is subject to adjustment dependent on the interest rate at various loan intervals during the loan term. The interest rate is gauged by the movement of a specified standard, such as the existing prime rate at the time of adjustment.

A variable rate mortgage may provide for balloon payments. This means that, although the loan is amortized over a longer period of time, e.g. thirty years, for the purpose of calculating a monthly payment, the loan actually becomes due and payable after a shorter period of time, such as five years, at which time the balloon payment—the entire indebtedness—must be paid.

Conventional Mortgage

Loans usually fall under the categories of conventional mortgages or governmental mortgages. A conventional mortgage is one which is made directly by the lender to the buyer with very few regulations or restrictions. Generally, a lender will require that an appraisal of the property is conducted so as to ensure that the property is worth the value being paid.

Governmental Mortgage

The most commonly sought governmental mortgages include the Federal Housing Administration (FHA) mortgages, which are insured, and the Veterans Administration (VA) mortgages, which are guaranteed. Governmental mortgages may contain strict restrictions on the mortgage terms and conditions.

FHA Mortgage

The Federal Housing Administration was established in 1934 to advance opportunities for Americans to own homes. By providing private lenders with mortgage insurance, the FHA gives them the security they need to lend to first-time buyers who might not be able to qualify for conventional loans. Anyone who meets the credit requirements, can afford the mortgage payments and cash investment, and who plans to use the mortgaged property as a primary residence may apply for an FHA-insured loan.

Because the FHA insures the loan, this is an incentive for the private lender to make the loan, particularly since FHA mortgages call for much lower downpayments, e.g., 95 to 97% loan to value financing. The FHA retains certain controls over approval of the mortgage. For example, the FHA makes its own appraisal of the property to make sure it meets their minimum standards. The FHA also places maximum limits on the mortgage amounts.

With the FHA, you don't need perfect credit or a high-paying job to qualify for a loan. The FHA also makes loans more accessible by requiring smaller down payments than conventional loans. In fact, an FHA down payment could be as little as a few months rent. And your monthly payments may not be much more than rent.

Lender claims paid by the FHA mortgage insurance program are drawn from the Mutual Mortgage Insurance fund. This fund is made up of premiums paid by FHA-insured loan borrowers. No tax dollars are used to fund the program.

FHA loan limits vary throughout the country, from $115,200 in low-cost areas to $208,800 in high-cost areas. The loan maximums for multi-unit homes are higher than those for single units and also vary by area. Because these maximums are linked to the conforming loan limit and average area home prices, FHA loan limits are periodically subject to change.

With the exception of a few additional forms, the FHA loan application process is similar to that of a conventional loan. You can apply for an FHA loan in person, via mail, telephone, the Internet, or in a video conference.

There is no minimum income requirement to qualify for an FHA loan. However, you must prove steady income for at least three years, and demonstrate that you've consistently paid your bills on time. Seasonal pay, child support, retirement pension payments, unemployment compensation, VA benefits, military pay, Social Security income, alimony, and rent paid by family all qualify as income sources. Part-time pay, overtime, and bonus pay also count as long as they are steady. Income type is not as important as income steadiness with the FHA.

VA Mortgage

As with FHA loans, under the VA mortgage program, private lenders are refunded the full amount of the guaranteed portion of the loan if the veteran defaults. The VA also requires its own appraisal of the property prior to the loan being made.

Secondary Market Mortgages

The government has also created a secondary mortgage market in which they buy first mortgages from various lenders. This frees the lender's finances so that they can make additional loans, and serves the public interest, particularly when the economic climate is not good. The most common secondary market purchasers are the Federal National Mortgage Association (FNMA)—commonly known as "Fannie Mae," the Government National Mortgage Association (GNMA)—commonly known as "Ginnie Mae," and the Federal Home Loan Mortgage Corporation (FHLMC)—commonly known as "Freddie Mac." Each particular purchaser has their own rules and requirements concerning the mortgages they are willing to buy.

THE CLOSING

The "closing" is the finalization of the real estate transaction. If the buyer has applied for financing, the closing takes place soon after the mortgage has been approved. The closing is usually held at the office of the attorney for one of the participants, e.g., the buyer, seller or lender.

At the closing, each of the parties finalizes their part of the agreement. The Buyer pays the purchase price of the property to the Seller, less any deposits already made. There are also adjustments based on items such as property taxes and utility bills for the time the seller held title to the property, which may have been paid by the seller, or which are payable by the seller. If the Buyer is financing part of the purchase price, the Lender will pay the loan proceeds to the Seller on the Buyer's behalf.

The Deed

The deed is the most common method of transferring ownership in real estate. At the closing, the deed is executed and turned over to the party who is responsible for its recording.

Legal Requirements

In order for a deed to be valid, it must meet several requirements, as set forth below.

(1) The seller of the property, also known as the grantor, must have the legal right to transfer the property and must sign the deed over to the buyer.

The grantor may be an individual, a partnership, a corporation, a governmental authority, or someone in a fiduciary capacity who has authority to transfer ownership of the property (such as a court order or a written and recorded agreement). Examples of fiduciaries are trustees, executors, and administrators.

(2) The buyer of the property, also known as the grantee, must be accurately identified, and the addresses for both the grantor and grantee must be stated.

(3) The deed must also specify the form of ownership which is being transferred, and the language of conveyance which expresses the intent to transfer the property.

(4) Another requirement for any valid contract, is the recital of consideration, i.e., the exchange of something of value by each party. In this case, consideration refers to the payment of a sum of money by the buyer, and the surrender of the deed to the property by the seller. The usual recital of consideration in a deed reads as follows:

> Witnesseth, that the party of the first part, in consideration of ten dollars and other valuable consideration paid by the party of the second part, does hereby grant and release unto the party of the second part. . .all that certain plot, piece or parcel of land. . .

The exact purchase price is generally not stated in the deed for confidentiality reasons. The fact that there is a recital of consideration suffices to satisfy the requirement.

(5) The deed must be delivered to, and accepted by, the grantee. This is evidenced by the payment of the purchase price in exchange for the deed.

(6) The signatures on the deed must be acknowledged by a notary public in order for the deed to be accepted for recording.

Types of Deeds

The most common types of deeds used to convey property include:

The Full Covenant and Warranty Deed

The full covenant and warranty deed is one in which the grantor fully warrants, or guarantees, that there is good title to the property. This guarantee dates back through the chain of title, and each prior grantor of a warranty deed may be liable to the buyer if a claim is made which is traced back to the date of conveyance by a particular prior grantor.

The Bargain and Sale Deed With Covenant

The bargain and sale deed with covenant is the simplest and most commonly used deed. It conveys all of the rights and interests that the grantor of the property holds. It also contains a covenant warranting good title to the property. However, unlike the full covenant and warranty deed, the bargain and sale covenant only relates to claims arising out of the period of ownership of the grantor who is conveying the deed.

The Bargain and Sale Deed Without Covenant

The bargain and sale deed without covenant does not contain the statement of warranty of title. It is similar to the quitclaim deed in that it does not protect the buyer from liens or other third party claims on the property should they arise. The difference between the quitclaim deed and the bargain and sale deed without covenant is that the latter contains language which, at the very least, implies that the grantor actually owns the property being conveyed.

The Quitclaim Deed

The quitclaim deed, like the bargain and sale deed without covenant, conveys all of the rights and interest that the grantor of the property holds, however, it does not contain language which implies that the grantor actually owns the property. Thus, if the grantor has no rights to the property, the grantee, in reality, receives nothing by way of the deed.

The Referee's Deed

The referee's deed is used to convey property by the referee following a foreclosure sale. Like the quitclaim deed, the referee's deed does not contain covenants warranting title.

The Executor's Deed

The executor's deed is used by the executor of a will to convey property of a decedent's estate. The executor's deed usually contains a covenant against the executor's acts, similar to the covenant against grantor's acts contained in the bargain and sale deed.

The Legal Description

The deed contains a legal description of the property which is the subject of the transaction. The legal description is based on a detailed survey of the property. It is important that the description be as accurate as possible so that the parties understand exactly what is being conveyed. There are three common types of legal descriptions used: (1) Metes and bounds; (2) Record plat; and (3) Rectangular.

(1) Metes and Bounds

Legal descriptions of properties were historically recorded in terms of "metes and bounds" by the settling colonies, hence the archaic language used in the description.

Metes refers to the actual measurement of the property, and bounds refers to the physical boundaries of the property. The property description details the direction of, and the distance between, physical points of reference. An example of a metes and bounds legal description is:

All that certain lot, piece or parcel of land, situate, lying and being in the Borough and County of Queens, City and State of New York, bounded and described as follows:

BEGINNING at a point on the northerly side of 30th Avenue, distance 150 feet westerly from the intersection formed by the northerly side of 30th Avenue and the westerly side of 88th Street;

RUNNING THENCE northerly parallel with 88th Street a distance of 100 feet;

THENCE westerly parallel with 30th Avenue for a distance of 50 feet;

THENCE southerly parallel with 30th Avenue a distance of 50 feet to the northerly side of 30th Avenue, and

THENCE easterly along the northerly side of 30th Avenue a distance of 20 feet to the point or place BEGINNING.

(2) Record Plat Descriptions

Record plat descriptions refers to the method of describing the property by lot and block, also incorporating the existing method of legal description into the detailed record plat.

(3) The Rectangular System

The rectangular system was adopted by Congress in 1785. This is the method used by the majority of states. The rectangular system uses a grid with lines running north and south—known as meridians—and lines running east and west—known as parallels. These lines create squares, each of which represents a certain distance within the town. The squares are divided and subdivided until the land within each section is identified.

Closing Costs

"Closing Costs" are additional costs the Buyer or Seller must pay in connection with closing the real estate transaction. The most common Buyer closing costs are detailed below, however, actual items and figures may vary depending on the particular transaction. The exact figures are provided to the buyer shortly before the closing takes place.

Common closing items include:

Title Insurance

Title insurance is an insurance policy which covers any losses resulting from any claims, defects, or encumbrances to the title which were not discovered during the title search. It does not cover any defects which were known to the title company and provided in the policy as exceptions to coverage. In most cases, when financing is involved, the lender will require any such defects to be cured prior to closing if the title insurer will not provide the necessary coverage to those items.

The insurance company is obligated to defend the insured's right against any claims which do not appear as exceptions in the policy, and to pay any losses incurred thereby. For example, if a third party makes a claim that they have some interest in the property, and sues on their claim, the title insurer is required to defend the insured in the lawsuit, and to either settle the claim, or pay any damages resulting from an unfavorable verdict.

Although a buyer is not required to purchase title insurance, it is recommended. Further, if the buyer is financing the purchase, the lender will require that, at the very least, the lender's interest in the property—to the extent of the amount of the mortgage—is covered by title insurance. The buyer also has the option to pay an additional premium to cover the difference between the mortgage amount and the purchase price. It is also wise to purchase—for a small additional fee—a market value rider. A market value rider provides that the property is covered up to the fair market value at the time the claim is made.

For example, if the purchase price of the property is $50,000, and the mortgage amount is $40,000, the lender will require that a title insurance policy is purchased indemnifying the lender up to $40,000. The buyer may pay an additional premium to have the property covered for the full purchase price of $50,000. However, if a claim is made ten years after the purchase, when the fair market value of the property is $200,000, the insured is only covered up to $50,000. Purchase of the market value rider would indemnify the insured up to the full market value at the time of the loss, which in this case is $200,000.

Loan Origination Fee

The loan origination fee is the service charge made by the lender for the granting of the loan. It is commonly referred to in terms of points, meaning a percentage point of the loan amount. For example, on a $100,000 loan, a one-point loan origination fee would be one thousand dollars.

Homeowner Insurance

A paid homeowner's insurance policy is a requirement for closing a mortgage. Newer homes and homes constructed with materials like brick tend to have lower premiums. Properties in flood plain areas generally require extra flood insurance. Obtain estimates from several insurance companies before you purchase your policy.

Miscellaneous Items

Other items commonly paid at closing include prepaid interest, which is charged by the lender from the date of closing until the end of the month; fees for the credit report and appraisal, if not already paid; and legal fees. The lender may also escrow 3 to 6 month's of property insurance premiums and tax payments, which are held by the lender until due and payable. In addition, premiums for private mortgage insurance (PMI) may be required by the lender if the loan to value ratio exceeds 80%. Such insurance may be required until the loan is reduced accordingly.

A schedule of estimated closing costs is set forth at Appendix 8.

THE LOAN PAYMENT

A loan payment is generally made up of the following:

Principal

The principal portion of the payment is that amount which goes towards reducing the actual amount you borrowed.

Interest

The interest portion of the payment represents the amount you pay to the lender for the money borrowed.

Homeowner Insurance

Most mortgage payments include an amount that is placed in escrow in order to pay the homeowner insurance premium. The insurance protects the homeowner and lender in case of damage to the property, i.e., caused by fire, theft, etc.

Property Taxes

Most mortgage payments include an amount that is placed in escrow in order to pay property taxes as they become due.

POST-CLOSING CONSIDERATIONS

Taking Possession

Following the closing, the buyers are generally entitled to take immediate possession of the house, unless some other arrangement has been made. If the seller is unable to immediately vacate the house, the contract usually provides for certain payments to be made to the buyers for each day the seller occupies the property after the closing. The contract usually requires the seller to turn over the property in a "broom-swept" condition. This generally means that the seller removes all personal property and debris from the premises.

Recording the Deed

Following the closing, the person responsible for recording the deed—usually the title company representative—files the deed, along with the required fee, with the appropriate authority. It is important that the deed be recorded as soon thereafter as practicable so as to give the public constructive notice of the transaction, and make the transfer part of the chain of title for that property. Because laws may vary, the reader is cautioned to check the recording requirements of their own jurisdiction to make sure that their rights are preserved.

CHAPTER 5:
FORECLOSURES

AVOIDING FORECLOSURE

If a borrower defaults on his or her mortgage payments, the lender may begin foreclosure proceedings. Foreclosure is the legal process of repossessing and taking ownership of a home. If your home is foreclosed upon, you must leave the house. If your property is subsequently sold for less than your mortgage loan balance, you may also be liable to the lender for the difference. This is known as a deficiency judgment.

Foreclosure negatively affects one's credit and stays on their credit report for a long period of time. Therefore, if you are in danger of defaulting on your mortgage, it is advisable to address the problem early on rather than wait until the lender has taken steps towards foreclosure.

Never ignore letters received from your lender. If you ignore the letters, the lender will take greater steps towards collecting the debt. If you explain your situation, the lender may be able to help. After all, foreclosure can be costly for the lender. If they know you are trying to rectify the situation, they will likely work with you and propose alternative repayment options. Available options may include:

Special Forbearance

The lender may be able to arrange a repayment plan based on your financial situation and provide for a temporary reduction or suspension of payments.

Refinance

You may be able to refinance the mortgage loan and/or extend the term of the loan, thus reducing your monthly payments to a more affordable level.

Sale

The lender may allow you to sell your property and pay your loan without foreclosure so you can avoid damaging your credit history. However, the lender will likely require that the sale take place within a short period of time.

Deed-in-lieu of Foreclosure

The lender may permit you to voluntarily surrender your property without going through the formal foreclosure procedure.

PURCHASING FORECLOSURES

When a borrower with a mortgage defaults on the payments, the lender—private or government—will foreclose on the property and take ownership. The lender will then list the property with an agent and attempt to sell the property at market value as quickly as possible to avoid incurring additional expenses in upkeep and maintenance of the property. The buyer usually takes the foreclosure property in an "as is" condition. Therefore, the buyer is advised to have a home inspection performed on the property before purchasing .

Lender-owned properties are available for purchase by the general public, including investors, provided they have the cash or can qualify for a mortgage to purchase the property. A prospective buyer can contact the foreclosure department of a lending institution to inquire as to whether they have any foreclosures on the market.

GOVERNMENT FORECLOSURES

As set forth below, two primary sources of government owned foreclosure properties are the U.S. Housing and Urban Development and the Veterans Administration.

Housing and Urban Development (HUD) Homes

When an individual with a HUD-insured mortgage defaults on his or her mortgage payments, the lender will foreclose upon the property. HUD then pays the lender what is owed and takes ownership of the property. HUD will establish the fair market value of the property and advertise the property for sale through a sealed-bid procedure. The bids are submitted through HUD-registered real estate brokers.

Like most foreclosures, HUD Homes are sold "as-is," without warranty. HUD does not make repairs nor does HUD pay the buyer to make any repairs. However, an estimate of the cost of the repairs will be reflected in a reduced list price. HUD also will pay all or a portion of the financing and closing costs, at the buyer's request. However, requesting such a reduction will also reduce the bid amount accordingly, and a higher bid amount will prevail.

HUD homes must be viewed in the presence of a HUD-registered broker. HUD maintains a list of their registered brokers. Once you have viewed the property, you can submit a bid through that broker. HUD homes are sold during their listing period. Once that period has ended, all submitted bids are opened and the highest bid will be accepted. If none of the submitted bids are accepted by HUD, the property will remain on the list of properties for sale. If your bid is successful, you are generally expected to close within 30-60 days. HUD will pay the selling agent's commission at closing.

HUD is not a lender. However, it does maintain a number of mortgage insurance programs which may help the buyer qualify for a loan through a HUD-approved lender.

Although HUD homes are primarily offered to individuals who intend to occupy the home as their primary residence, unsold properties may become available to investors. Prospective investors should contact HUD for more details.

Veterans Administration (VA) Homes

When someone with a VA-insured mortgage defaults on their payments, the lender forecloses on the home and the VA pays the lender what is owed and takes ownership of the property. The VA then sells the property at market value.

A foreclosed VA home is available for sale to both veterans and non-veterans, whether they are owner-occupants or investors. As with HUD homes, VA homes are also sold on an "as-is" basis, with no warranty. However, the VA will also adjust its asking price to reflect the estimated cost of repairs. The VA will also pay all or most of the financing and closing costs.

You must view a VA home with a VA-registered real estate agent, who will submit a bid for you during the competitive bid period. At the end of the period, all offers are opened and the highest bid is generally the one which is accepted. If the property is not sold during the bid period, it remains on the market and an offer can be submitted at any time thereafter.

As with a HUD home, if you are a successful bidder on a VA property, you must generally close within 30-60 days from the date your offer is accepted. The VA pays the selling agent's commission at closing.

CHAPTER 6:
MANUFACTURED HOUSING

IN GENERAL

In recent years, nearly one-third of all new single-family homes bought have been manufactured homes. The term "manufactured home" was adopted in 1980 by Congress to describe a type of house that is built in the controlled environment of a manufacturing plant and transported in one or more sections.

Manufactured homes were formerly known as "mobile homes." However, "mobile" is no longer applicable insofar as less than five percent of manufactured homes are ever moved off of their original site.

THE MANUFACTURED HOME CONSTRUCTION AND SAFETY STANDARDS

The sale of a manufactured home is regulated by the federal government. By an Act of Congress in 1974, the U.S. Department of Housing and Urban Development (HUD) was designated as the government agency responsible for overseeing the Federal Manufactured Housing Program. The Act gives HUD broad investigatory authority to conduct inspections, issue subpoenas and issue orders. HUD may bring administrative actions against manufacturers or inspection agencies for violations of the Act or regulations. The Act also provides for injunctive actions in Federal court and civil money penalties and criminal sanctions.

The Manufactured Housing program was established to protect the health and safety of the owners of manufactured homes. The intent of the program is to reduce personal injuries, deaths, property damage, and insurance costs associated with manufactured homes, and to improve the quality and durability of the homes.

A manufactured home must be built to conform with the Manufactured Home Construction and Safety Standards—a building code developed by HUD. The home must be built in dwelling units of at least 320 square feet in size with a permanent chassis to assure the initial and continued transportability of the home. The home must also display a red certification label on the exterior of each transportable section. HUD standards cover body and frame requirements, thermal protection, plumbing, electrical, fire safety and other aspects of the home.

Selected provisions of the National Manufactured Home Construction and Safety Standards Act are set forth at Appendix 9.

HUD oversees the enforcement of the construction standards working through private inspection agencies and State governments. The agency within HUD that is responsible for the oversight function is the Office of Consumer and Regulatory Affairs, Manufactured Housing and Standards Division.

If a manufactured home does not conform to Federal standards, the manufacturer may be required to notify the consumer. If the home contains a defect which presents an unreasonable risk of injury or death, the manufacturer may be required to correct the defect.

ALTERATIONS

Retailers may make alterations to manufactured houses, but those alterations must comply with the standards. If an alteration does not comply with the standards, the home cannot be sold or offered for sale.

An alteration is defined as the replacement, addition, modification, or removal of any equipment or installation, after sale by a manufacturer to a retailer, but prior to sale by the retailer to a purchaser, that may affect the construction, fire safety, occupancy, or plumbing, heating, or electrical systems of the home.

INSTALLATION

Installation is one of the most important elements of purchasing a new manufactured home. The installer is generally the retailer, or someone under contract with the retailer performs the installation. The purchaser should make sure the contractor installs the home in accordance with the manufacturer's instructions and, if applicable, state installation regulations.

When installing a manufactured home, the following items must be considered:

(1) locality's requirements for zoning, septic, electrical and/or building permits;

(2) site preparation and access to the site;

(3) stable soil and proper foundation system, including the anchoring system, that is approved/listed for use in the proper class of soil;

(4) a perimeter enclosure may be either recommended or required; and

(5) utility hook-ups and dryer vent discharge, as addressed in the installation manual provided with the home.

The consumer should always check with the retailer and state or local building officials concerning the installation of a manufactured home.

WARRANTIES

Most manufacturers offer a warranty that covers the performance of the structure and factory-installed plumbing, heating, and electrical systems during a specified warranty period, and some states require warranties under state law. Factory-installed appliances and certain building components may be covered under their own warranties.

Prior to purchasing a manufactured home, inquire as to who will guarantee the warranty and who performs the repairs. Make sure you get a written list of the items that are covered under the warranty. In general, the manufacturer is not responsible for normal wear and tear, consumer abuse and/or neglect, and improper installation. In addition to any written warranty offered by the manufacturer, you may have certain "implied warranties" when you buy a manufactured home. An implied warranty is an unspoken, unwritten promise that a product is fit to be sold and used for its intended purposes—i.e., to be inhabited. These implied warranties protect you even if no written warranty is offered by the manufacturer or retailer. Most states allow "as-is" sales that exclude implied warranties. However, some states do not permit a seller to exclude or limit implied warranties.

CONSUMER COMPLAINTS

HUD has entered into cooperative agreements with 36 State governments to conduct periodic checks of plant records and to respond to consumer complaints. These State governments each designate a State Administrative Agency (SAA) to carry out this program. The HUD standards preempt State and local laws which are not identical to the Federal standards.

A directory of state administrative agencies that administer the HUD manufactured housing program is set forth at Appendix 10.

HUD staff carries out these functions in the 14 states that have not entered into an agreement with HUD. HUD's mailing address and contact information is:

Manufactured Housing and Standards Division
Office of Consumer and Regulatory Affairs
Department of Housing and Urban Development
451 7th St. SW, Room 9152
Washington, D.C. 20410-8000
(Tel): 1-800-927-2891/(Fax): 202-708-4213/(E-mail): mhs@hud.gov.

If a consumer has a complaint about the performance of their manufactured home that has not been resolved by the retailer who sold the unit, or by the manufacturer that built the home, he or she should contact the SAA in their state. Consumers in Alaska, Connecticut, Delaware, Hawaii, Illinois, Kansas, Massachusetts, Montana, New Hampshire, North Dakota, Ohio, Oklahoma, Vermont and Wyoming—the 14 states without an SAA—should contact HUD.

When making the complaint, the consumer should provide the following information:

1. Name, address and telephone number;

2. The name of the manufacturer;

3. The serial and model number of the home;

4. The label number on the red tag located on the back of the home;

5. The date purchased;

6. A description of the problem;

7. Copies of any correspondence with the retailer and the manufacturer concerning the problem.

FINANCING A MANUFACTURED HOME

There are many alternatives for financing a manufactured home. The most common method of financing a manufactured home is through a retail installment contract available through the retailer. A growing number of lending institutions are providing conventional and government-insured financing plans for prospective manufactured home owners. Some lending institutions that offer conventional, long-term real estate mortgages may require the homes to be placed on approved foundations.

Manufactured homes are eligible for government-insured loans offered by the U.S. Department of Housing and Urban Development (HUD), the Federal Housing Administration (FHA), the Veterans Administration (VA), and the Rural Housing Services (RHS) under the U.S. Department of Agriculture.

Under the HUD/FHA Title I Manufactured Home Loan program, approved lenders loan funds to eligible borrowers to purchase manufactured homes. Credit is granted based on the applicant's credit history and ability to repay the loan in regular monthly payments. Title I loans are not government loans nor are they low interest loans. However, HUD/FHA does insure the loan in case the borrower defaults.

The Title I loan may be used for the purchase or refinancing of a manufactured home, a developed lot on which to place a manufactured home, or both. The home must be used as the primary residence of the borrowers.

The insured loan is limited to a maximum of $48,600 for the manufactured home only; $16,200 for the developed lot on which to place a manufactured home; and $64,800 for the manufactured home and lot. The loan term may not exceed 20 years for a manufactured home only. The lot loans are limited to 15 years. A loan on a single-module home and lot is limited to 20 years, while a loan on a multi-module home and lot can extend to 25 years.

A loan on a new manufactured home requires a minimum cash downpayment of five percent of the first $5,000 of the purchase price and 10 percent of the balance. The same downpayment is required on all combination loans, whether the home is new or existing. The minimum downpayment on an existing manufactured home loan or a manufactured home lot loan is 10 percent of the purchase price.

The interest rate is a fixed rate which is generally based upon the prevailing market rate in the area at the time the loan is made. The loan must be secured by a first lien on the manufactured home/and or lot and on any furnishings, equipment, or appurtenances being financed with the loan.

CHAPTER 7:
HOUSING DISCRIMINATION

THE FAIR HOUSING ACT

In response to evidence of continuing housing discrimination, Congress passed the Fair Housing Act Amendments of 1988 to provide for more effective enforcement of fair housing rights through judicial and administrative avenues and to expand the number of protected classes covered under Federal fair housing laws.

Selected provisions of The Fair Housing Act are set forth at Appendix 11.

Under the Fair Housing Act, it is illegal for any individual to discriminate against any person based on race; color; national origin; religion; gender; disability; or familial status. In general, discrimination in housing occurs when someone:

1. Refuses to rent to you or sell you housing;

2. Tells you housing is unavailable when in fact it is available;

3. Shows you apartments or homes in certain neighborhoods only;

4. Advertises housing to preferred groups of people only;.

5. Refuses to provide you with information regarding mortgage loans, denies you a mortgage loan, or imposes different terms or conditions on a mortgage loan;

6. Denies you property insurance;

7. Conducts property appraisals in a discriminatory manner;

8. Refuses to make certain modifications or accommodations for persons with a mental or physical disability, including persons recovering from alcohol and substance abuse, and HIV/AIDS-related illnesses;

9. Fails to design and construct housing in an accessible manner;

10. Harasses, coerces, intimidates, or interferes with anyone exercising or assisting someone else with their fair housing rights.

---

11. Advertises or makes any statement that indicates a limitation or preference based on race, color, national origin, religion, sex, familial status, or handicap. This prohibition against discriminatory advertising also applies to single-family and owner-occupied housing that is otherwise exempt from the Fair Housing Act.

Persons that may not discriminate include, but are not limited to:

1. Landlords;

2. Resident managers or assistant resident managers;

3. Apartment maintenance crew or other staff;

4. Property managers;

5. Property owners;

6. Newspapers or other sources of advertisement;

7. Real estate agents;

8. Lenders or other financial institutions;

9. Insurance agents or companies;

10. Appraisers;

11. Builders;

12. Architects; and

13. Any other person who designs, constructs or provides housing.

Exemptions

The Fair Housing Act covers most housing. In some circumstances, the Act exempts owner-occupied buildings with no more than four units, single-family housing sold or rented without the use of a broker, and housing operated by organizations and private clubs that limit occupancy to members.

Housing for older persons is exempt from the prohibition against familial status discrimination if:

1. The HUD Secretary has determined that it is specifically designed for and occupied by elderly persons under a Federal, State or local government program; or

2. It is occupied solely by persons who are 62 or older; or

3. It houses at least one person who is 55 or older in at least 80 percent of the occupied units and adheres to a policy that demonstrates an intent to house persons who are 55 or older.

Nevertheless, a transition period permits residents on or before September 13, 1988, to continue living in the housing, regardless of their age, without interfering with the exemption.

Unless a building or community qualifies as housing for older persons, it may not discriminate based on familial status. That is, it may not discriminate against families in which one or more children under 18 live with a parent; a person who has legal custody of the child or children; or the designee of the parent or legal custodian with the parent or custodian's written permission. Familial status protection also applies to pregnant women and anyone securing legal custody of a child under 18.

Accessibility Requirements for Disabled Persons

In buildings that were ready for first occupancy after March 13, 1991, and have an elevator and four or more units:

1. Public and common areas must be accessible to persons with disabilities;

2. Doors and hallways must be wide enough for wheelchairs;

3. All units must have:

(a) An accessible route into and through the unit ;

(b) Accessible light switches, electrical outlets, thermostats and other environmental controls;

(c) Reinforced bathroom walls to allow later installation of grab bars; and

(d) Kitchens and bathrooms that can be used by people in wheelchairs.

If a building with four or more units has no elevator and was ready for first occupancy after March 13, 1991, these standards apply to ground floor units.

These requirements for new buildings do not replace any more stringent standards in State or local law.

CONSUMER COMPLAINTS

If you believe you are the victim of housing discrimination, and that you are being excluded from a neighborhood or particular house, immediately contact the U.S. Department of Housing and Urban Development (HUD). Also, contact HUD if you believe you are being discriminated against on the basis of race, color, religion, sex, nationality, familial status, or disability. HUD's Office of Fair Housing has a hotline for reporting incidents of discrimination: (TEL) 1-800-669-9777/(TTY) 1-800-927-9275.

A Directory of HUD Fair Housing Enforcement Centers is set forth at Appendix 12.

You have one year after an alleged violation to file a complaint with HUD, but you should file it as soon as possible. When filing a complaint with HUD, you should include:

1. Your name and address;

2. The name and address of the person your complaint is against—known as "the respondent";

3. The address or other identification of the housing involved;

4. A short description of the alleged violation, i.e., the event that caused you to believe your rights were violated; and

5. The date of the alleged violation.

A sample HUD Housing Discrimination Complaint Form is set forth at Appendix 13.

HUD will notify you when it receives your complaint. In investigating the complaint, HUD will:

1. Notify the alleged violator of your complaint and permit that person to submit an answer;

2. Investigate your complaint and determine whether there is reasonable cause to believe the Fair Housing Act has been violated; and

3. Notify you if it cannot complete an investigation within 100 days of receiving your complaint.

HUD will try to reach a conciliation agreement with the respondent. A conciliation agreement must protect both you and the public interest. If an agreement is signed, HUD will take no further action on your complaint. However, if HUD has reasonable cause to believe that a conciliation agreement is breached, HUD will recommend that the Attorney General file suit.

If HUD has determined that your State or local agency has the same fair housing powers as HUD, HUD will refer your complaint to that agency for investigation and notify you of the referral. That agency must begin work on your complaint within 30 days or HUD may take it back.

If your case goes to an administrative hearing, HUD attorneys will litigate the case on your behalf. You may intervene in the case and be represented by your own attorney if you wish. An Administrative Law Judge will consider evidence from you and the respondent. If the judge decides that discrimination occurred, the respondent can be ordered to take the following actions:

1. Compensate you for actual damages, including humiliation, pain and suffering;

2. Provide injunctive or other equitable relief, for example, to make the housing available to you;

3. Pay the Federal Government a civil penalty to vindicate the public interest. The maximum penalties are $10,000 for a first violation and $50,000 for a third violation within seven years.

4. Pay reasonable attorney's fees and costs.

If you or the respondent choose to have your case decided in Federal District Court, the Attorney General will file a suit and litigate it on your behalf. The District Court can also order relief, and award actual damages, attorney's fees and costs. In addition, the court can award punitive damages.

You may file suit, at your expense, in Federal District Court or state court within two years of an alleged violation. If you cannot afford an attorney, the Court may appoint one for you. You may bring suit even after filing a complaint, if you have not signed a conciliation agreement and an Administrative Law Judge has not started a hearing. A court may award actual and punitive damages and attorney's fees and costs.

APPENDIX 1:
SAMPLE AGENCY DISCLOSURE AND ACKNOWLEDGMENT FORM REGARDING REAL ESTATE AGENCY RELATIONSHIPS

Before you enter into a discussion with a real estate agent regarding a real estate transaction, you should understand what type of agency relationship you wish to have with that agent.

New York State law requires real estate licensees who are acting as agents of buyers or sellers of property to advise the potential buyers or sellers with whom they work of the nature of their agency relationship and the rights and obligations it creates.

SELLER'S AGENT

If you are interested in selling real property, you can engage a real estate agent as a seller's agent. A seller's agent, including a listing agent under a listing agreement with the seller, acts solely on behalf of the seller. You can authorize a seller's agent to do other things including the right to hire subagents, broker's agents or work with other agents such as buyer's agents on a cooperative basis. A subagent or "cooperating agent" is one who has agreed to work with the seller's agent, often through a multiple listing service. A subagent may work in a different real estate office.

A seller's agent has, without limitation, the following fiduciary duties to the seller: reasonable care, undivided loyalty, confidentiality, full disclosure, obedience, and a duty to account.

The obligations of an agent are also subject to any specific provision set forth in an agreement between the agent and the seller.

In dealing with the buyer, a seller's agent should:

(a) exercise reasonable skill and care in performance of the agent's duties;

(b) deal honestly, fairly and in good faith; and

(c) disclose all facts known to the agent materially affecting the value or desirability of property, except as otherwise provided by law.

BUYER'S AGENT

If you are interested in buying real property, you can engage a real estate agent as a buyer's agent. A buyer's agent acts solely on behalf of the buyer. You can authorize a buyer's agent to do other things including the right to hire subagents, broker's agents or work with other agents, such as a seller's agents, on a cooperative basis.

A buyer's agent has, without limitation, the following fiduciary duties to the buyer: reasonable care, undivided loyalty confidentiality, full disclosure, obedience and a duty to account.

The obligations of an agent are also subject to any specific provisions set forth in an agreement between the agent and the buyer.

In dealing with the seller, a buyer's agent should:

(a) exercise reasonable care in performance of the agent's duties;

(b) deal honestly, fairly and in good faith;

(c) disclose all facts known to the agent materially affecting the value or the desirability of the property; and

(d) disclose all facts known to the agent materially affecting the value or desirability of the property, except as otherwise provided by law.

DUAL AGENCY

A real estate agent acting directly or through an associated licensee can be the agent of both the seller and the buyer in a transaction, but only with the knowledge and informed consent in writing of both the seller and the buyer.

In such a dual agency situation, the agent will not be able to provide the full range of fiduciary duties to the buyer and seller.

The obligation of an agent is also subject to any specific provisions set forth in an agreement between the agent and the buyer and seller.

An agent acting as a dual agent must explain carefully to both the buyer and seller that the agent is acting for the other party as well. The agent should also explain the possible effects of dual representation, including that by consenting to the dual agency relationship, the buyer and seller are giving up their right to undivided loyalty.

A BUYER OR SELLER SHOULD CAREFULLY CONSIDER THE POSSIBLE CONSEQUENCES OF A DUAL AGENCY RELATIONSHIP BEFORE AGREEING TO SUCH REPRESENTATION

GENERAL CONSIDERATIONS

You should carefully read all agreements to ensure that they adequately express your understanding of the transaction. A real estate agent is a person qualified to advise about real estate. If legal, tax or other advice is desired, consult a competent professional in that field.

Throughout the transaction, you may receive more than one disclosure form. The law requires each agent assisting in the transaction to represent you with this disclosure form. You should read its contents each time it is presented to you, considering the relationship between you and the real estate agent in your specific transaction.

ACKNOWLEDGMENT OF PROSPECTIVE BUYER

(1) I have received, read and understand this disclosure notice.

(2) I understand that a seller's agent, including a listing agent, is the agent of the seller exclusively, unless the seller and buyer otherwise agree.

(3) I understand that subagents, including subagents participating in a multiple listing service, are agents of the seller exclusively.

(4) I understand that I may engage my own agent to be my buyer's broker.

(5) I understand that the agent presenting this form to me,_____ _____ of _____ is:

(check applicable relationship)

_____ an agent of the seller

_____ my agent as a buyer's agent

Dated:_____ Buyer:_____

Dated:_____ Buyer:_____

ACKNOWLEDGMENT OF PROSPECTIVE SELLER

(1) I have received, read and understand this disclosure notice.

(2) I understand that a seller's agent, including a listing agent, is the agent of the seller exclusively, unless the seller and buyer otherwise agree.

(3) I understand that subagents, including subagents participating in a multiple listing service, are agents of the seller exclusively.

(4) I understand that a buyer's agent is an agent of the buyer exclusively.

(5) I understand that the agent presenting this form to me,_____
_____ of _____ is:

(check applicable relationship)

_____ my agent as a seller's agent
_____ an agent of the buyer

Dated:_____ Seller:_____
Dated:_____ Seller:_____

ACKNOWLEDGMENT OF PROSPECTIVE BUYER AND SELLER TO DUAL AGENCY

(1) I have received, read and understand this disclosure notice.

(2) I understand that a dual agent will be working for both the seller and the buyer.

(3) I understand that I may engage my own agent as a seller's agent or a buyer's agent.

(4) I understand that I am giving up my right to the agent's undivided loyalty.

(5) I have carefully considered the possible consequences of a dual agency relationship.

I understand that the agent presenting this form to me,_____
_____ of _____ is a dual agent working for both the buyer and seller, acting as such with consent of both buyer and seller and following full disclosure to the buyer and seller.

Dated:_____ Seller:_____
Dated:_____ Seller:_____
Dated:_____ Buyer:_____
Dated:_____ Buyer:_____

ACKNOWLEDGMENT OF THE PARTIES TO THE CONTRACT

(1) I have received, read and understand this disclosure notice.

(2) I understand that the agent presenting this form to me,_____
_____ of _____ is:

(check applicable relationship)

_____ an agent of the seller

_____ an agent of the buyer

_____ a dual agent working for both the buyer and seller, acting as such with the consent of both buyer and seller and following full disclosure to the buyer and seller.

(3) I also understand that _____ of
_____ is:

_____ an agent of the seller

_____ an agent of the buyer

_____ a dual agent working for both the buyer and seller, acting as such with the consent of both buyer and seller and following full disclosure to the buyer and seller.

Dated:_____ Seller:_____

Dated:_____ Seller:_____

Dated:_____ Buyer:_____

Dated:_____ Buyer:_____

APPENDIX 2:
MODEL LICENSING LAW AS PROMULGATED BY THE NATIONAL ASSOCIATION OF REAL ESTATE LICENSE LAW OFFICIALS (NARELLO)

(1) Educational Requirement. State educational requirements for licensing vary from none to an accredited college or university degree. Most states impose a requirement of a high school diploma and a minimum number of classroom hours in real estate education.

(2) Experience Requirement (this requirement is limited to broker licenses). Most states require 2 years experience as a salesperson or 2 years experience in the real estate field as a prerequisite for licensing as a broker. The requirement of experience is coupled, in many states, with classes taken at an accredited college or university in real estate topics.

(3) Examination Requirement. All states require both salespersons and brokers to pass examinations to obtain licensing. More than half of the states use a standardized test accompanied by an additional section that covers laws and practices of the particular state. Examinations for brokers cover significantly more material than examinations for salespersons.

(4) Sponsorship Requirement. About half of the states require candidates for salespersons licenses to be sponsored by a licensed broker who will be responsible for the salesperson when the license is awarded.

(5) Minimum Age Requirement. In most states the minimum age for licensure is the age of majority in the state. In some states the minimum age for brokers may be higher than the minimum age for salespersons.

(6) Citizenship Requirement. Some states still require United States citizenship status as a prerequisite for licensing; however, this requirement

with respect to other forms of licensing has been struck down on constitutional grounds.

(7) Residency Requirement. Some states require that license applicants be residents of the state for 30 to 90 days before the application may be made. Again, such requirements for other licenses have been subject to constitutional challenges.

(8) Criminal Record Prohibition. Nearly all of the states have provisions prohibiting licensing if the applicant has been convicted of a felony. However, these states usually restrict the length of time for which a license may be denied on this basis.

(9) Application Requirements. All states require potential licensees to submit a completed form provided and developed by the regulating agency. Completion and delivery of the form to the agency is required 30 to 60 days prior to examination. Commonly, the application will require the applicant to give character references from persons in the community or from persons already established in the real estate business.

(10) Fee Requirements. All states require the payment of a licensing fee upon original application. Furthermore, a renewal fee is required to be paid at intervals established by the states.*

---

*   Source: Jennings, Marianne M., Real Estate Law, Kent Publishing Company, 1985.

APPENDIX 3:
SAMPLE BROKER/SALESPERSON
INDEPENDENT CONTRACTOR AGREEMENT

AGREEMENT

AGREEMENT made this 15th day of January, 2000, by and between John Doe, residing at 123 Main Street, New York, New York (hereinafter referred to as the "Salesperson") and ABC Real Estate, Inc., having a principal place of business at 456 North Avenue, New York, New York, (hereinafter referred to as the "Broker").

WITNESSETH:

WHEREAS, Salesperson and Broker are each respectively duly licensed pursuant to Article 12-A of the Real Property Law of the State of New York, and

WHEREAS, the parties hereto have freely and voluntarily entered into this Agreement, without duress.

NOW, THEREFORE, in consideration of the mutual promises herein contained, it is hereby agreed as follows:

(1) Salesperson is engaged as an independent contractor associated with the Broker pursuant to Article 12-A of the Real Property Law and shall be treated as such for all purposes, including but not limited to Federal and State income taxation, withholding tax regulations, unemployment insurance, and worker's compensation coverage.

(2) Salesperson shall:

(a) be paid a commission on Salesperson's gross sales, if any, without deduction for taxes, which commission shall be directly related to sales or other output;

(b) not be entitled to a draw against commissions;

(c) not receive any remuneration related to the number of hours worked; and

(d) not be treated as an employee with respect to such services for Federal and State income tax purposes.

(3) Salesperson shall be permitted to work such hours as Salesperson may elect to work.

(4) Salesperson shall be permitted to work out of Salesperson's residence or the offices of Broker or any other location in the sole discretion of Salesperson.

(5) Salesperson shall be free to engage in outside employment.

(6) Broker may provide office facilities and supplies for the use of Salesperson. All other expenses, including but not limited to automobile, travel, and entertainment expenses shall be borne by Salesperson.

(7) Broker may offer initial training and hold periodic sales meetings. The attendance by Salesperson at such sessions shall be at the option of Salesperson.

(8) Broker may offer a group insurance plan, and if Salesperson wishes to participate therein, all premiums shall be paid by Salesperson.

(9) Broker may elect, but shall be under no obligation, to assign leads to Salesperson on a rotating basis. Salesperson shall be responsible for procuring Salesperson's own leads.

(10) Broker and Salesperson shall comply with the requirements of Article 12-A of the Real Property Law and the regulations pertaining thereto. Such compliance shall not affect Salesperson's status as an independent contractor nor shall such compliance be construed as an indication that Salesperson is an employee of Broker for any purpose whatsoever.

(11) This contract and the association created thereby may be terminated by either party hereto at any time upon notice given by one party to the other.

(12) For purposes of this Agreement, the term "Broker" shall include individual real estate brokers, real estate brokerage companies, real estate brokerage corporations and any other entity acting as a principal broker, and the term "Salesperson" shall include real estate sales agents, and real estate brokers, who, as real estate licensees, associate with and place their real estate license with a principal broker.

(13) This Agreement shall be governed and construed in accordance with the laws of the State of New York.

(14) No waiver of any of the provisions of this Agreement or any of the rights or remedies of the parties hereto shall be valid unless such waiver is in writing, signed by the party to be charged therewith.

(15) Whenever in this Agreement any notices are required to be given, such notices shall be in writing and shall be sent by registered mail or certified mail, return receipt requested, to the party entitled to receive the same.

This Agreement and all of its terms, covenants and provisions insofar as applicable, shall be binding upon and inure to the benefit of the parties hereto, their respective heirs, executors, administrators, successors and assigns.

IN WITNESS WHEREOF, the individual parties hereto have hereunto set their hands and seals, and any corporate party has caused this instrument to be signed by a corporate officer and caused its corporate seal to be hereunto affixed, all as of the day and year first above written.

By:_____

    John Doe, Salesperson

By:_____

    Mary Smith, President
    ABC Real Estate, Inc., Broker

STATE OF NEW YORK)

COUNTY OF WESTCHESTER)

On the 15th day of January, 2000, before me personally came John Doe, to me known to be the individual described in, and who executed the foregoing instrument, and acknowledged that he executed the same.

_____

    Notary Public

STATE OF NEW YORK)

COUNTY OF WESTCHESTER)

On the 15th day of January, 2000, before me personally came Mary Smith, to me known, who being by me duly sworn, did depose and say that she is the President of ABC Real Estate, Inc., the corporation described in and which executed the foregoing instrument; that she knows the seal of said corporation; that the seal affixed to said instrument is such corporation seal; that it was so affixed by order of the Board of Directors of said corporation, and that she signed her name thereto by like order.*

Notary Public

---

*   Source: Westchester County Board of Realtors, Inc.

APPENDIX 4:
DIRECTORY OF MAJOR REAL ESTATE ASSOCIATIONS

NATIONAL ASSOCIATION OF REALTORS (NAR)
430 North Michigan Avenue
Chicago, IL 60611
312-329-8200

NAR is a membership organization. Membership is achieved by joining a local or state board. NAR defines a Realtor as a professional who subscribes to a strict code of ethics. NAR offers three professional designations: Realtor; Associate; and Graduate, Realtors Institute (GRI).

NATIONAL ASSOCIATION OF HOME BUILDERS (NAHB)
15th and M Streets NW
Washington, DC 20005
202-822-0200

NAHB is a membership organization. Its members are single family and apartment builders, brokers, and managers. NAHB disseminates information, and holds national conventions and meetings. NAHB offers two professional designations: Residential Apartment Manager (RAM) and Member of the Institute of Residential Marketing (MIRM).

REALTORS NATIONAL MARKETING INSTITUTE (RNMI)
430 North Michigan Avenue
Chicago, IL 6061
312-670-3780

RNMI promotes the professional standing of Realtors by providing practical education and advocating sound and ethical practices. RNMI offers three professional designations: Certified Real Estate Brokerage Manager (CRB); Certified Residential Salesman (CRS); and Certified Commercial Investment Member (CCIM).

INSTITUTE OF REAL ESTATE MANAGEMENT (IREM)
430 North Michigan Avenue
Chicago, IL 60611
312-329-8501

IREM serves the professional needs of property managers and disseminates useful property management information. IREM offers three professional designations: Certified Property Manager (CPM); Accredited Resident Manager (ARM); and Accredited Management Organization (AMO).

BUILDING OWNERS AND MANAGERS ASSOCIATION (BOMA)
1221 Massachusetts Avenue NW
Washington, DC 20005
202-289-7000

BOMA is a national membership organization for managers of commercial property which functions through local chapters in major cities. It is designed to increase professionalism and disseminate information. It is known for its annual experience exchange report and other economic statistics and sponsors its certification affiliate, Building Owners and Managers Institute International (BOMI). BOMI offers one professional designation: Real Property Administrator (RPA).

AMERICAN INSTITUTE OF REAL ESTATE APPRAISERS (AIREA)
430 North Michigan Avenue
Chicago, IL 60611
312-239-8559

AIREA establishes standards of professionalism and competence in appraisal activity, and trains and tests professional appraisers. AIREA offers two professional designations: Member, Appraisal Institute (MAI) and Residential Member (RM).

SOCIETY OF REAL ESTATE APPRAISERS
225 North Michigan Avenue
Chicago, IL 60611
312-819-2400

The Society of Real Estate Appraisers is a large membership organization established to promote professionalism and education for real estate appraisers and analysts. It establishes standards of performance and ethical conduct and offers three professional designations: Senior Residential Appraiser (SRA); Senior Real Property Appraiser (SRPA); and Senior Real Estate Analyst (SREA).

INTERNATIONAL COUNCIL OF SHOPPING CENTERS (ICSC)
665 Fifth Avenue
New York, NY 10022
212-421-8181

ICSC is a membership organization for shopping center developers, marketers, managers, and other shopping center professionals. It engages in wide-ranging educational activities for members, disseminates information and the products of its own research, and sponsors conventions, conferences, "colleges," and meetings. ICSC offers two professional designations: Accredited Shopping Center Promotion Director (ASPD) and Certified Shopping Center Manager (CSM).

INTERNATIONAL ASSOCIATION OF CORPORATE REAL ESTATE
EXECUTIVES (NACORE)
471 Spencer Drive South
West Palm Beach, FL 33409
305-683-811

NACORE is a national membership organization for corporate real estate officers. It disseminates information and offers numerous seminars and conferences.

MORTGAGE BANKERS ASSOCIATIONS OF AMERICA (MBA)
1125 15th Street NW
Washington, DC 20005
202-861-6500

MBA is a national membership organization that includes mortgage bankers and brokers as well as many institutional lenders. It operates through local chapters organized in cities throughout the country. It is designed to improve professionalism in real estate finance. It engages in research and political activity in its members' interests, and publishes a national monthly: The Mortgage Banker. MBA offers one professional designation: Certified Mortgage Banker (CMB).

REAL ESTATE SECURITIES AND SYNDICATION INSTITUTE (RESSI)
430 North Michigan Avenue
Chicago, IL 60611
312-670-6760

RESSI establishes professional standards of practice and offers educational courses. RESSI offers one professional designation: Certified Real Estate Securities Sponsor (CRSS).

SOCIETY OF INDUSTRIAL REALTORS OF THE NATIONAL
  ASSOCIATION OF REALTORS (SIR)
777 14th Street NW
Washington, DC 20005
202-383-1150

SIR unites those Realtors who buy, sell, or lease land or buildings to industry; fosters knowledge, education, integrity, and quality workmanship in industry real estate; and exchanges information and listings. SIR offers four professional designations: SIR, Active; SIR, Salesman Affiliate; SIR, Associate; and SIR, International Associate.*

---

*   Source: Westchester County Board of Realtors, Inc.

APPENDIX 5:
SAMPLE EXCLUSIVE AGENCY AGREEMENT

EXCLUSIVE AGENCY AGREEMENT

THIS AGREEMENT is effective _____, 20____, and confirms that _____ (Owner) has appointed _____ to act as Agent for the sale of property known as _____ in the State of New York.

In return for the Agent's agreement to use Agent's best efforts to sell the above property, the Owner agrees to grant the Agent an exclusive agency to sell this property under the following terms and conditions:

PERIOD OF AGREEMENT

(1) This agreement shall be effective from the above date and shall expire at midnight on _____, 19____.

PRICE AT WHICH PROPERTY WILL BE OFFERED AND AUTHORITY

(2) The property will be offered for sale at a list price of _____ and shall be sold, subject to negotiation, at such price and upon such terms to which Owner may agree. The word Owner refers to each and all parties who have ownership interest in the property and the undersigned represents they are the sole and exclusive owners and are fully authorized to enter into this agreement.

COMMISSION TO BE PAID AGENT

(3) The Agent shall be entitled to and Owner shall pay to Agent one commission of _____ of the selling price. Both the Owner and Agent ac-

---

knowledge that the above commission rate was not suggested nor influenced by anyone other than the parties to this Agreement. Owner hereby authorizes Agent to make an offer of cooperation to any other licensed real estate broker with whom Agent wishes to cooperate. Any commission due for a sale brought about by a Sub-Agent (another broker who is authorized by Agent to assist in the sale of Owner's property) or to an authorized Buyer's Agent shall be paid by the Agent from the commission received by the Agent pursuant to this Paragraph.

The commission offered by Agent to Sub-Agents shall be ____ of the gross selling price. The commission offered by Agent to Buyer's Agent shall be ____ of the gross selling price.

In the event that Owner authorizes Agent to compensate a Buyer's Agent, Owner acknowledges Owner's understanding that such Buyer's Agent is not representing Owner as Sub-Agent and that the Buyer's Agent will be representing only the interests of the prospective purchaser.

Owner will not be obligated to pay a commission to Agent if Owner sells Owner's property without the efforts of either Agent, any Sub-Agent or a Buyer's Agent whose services have been authorized by Agent.

OWNER'S OBLIGATIONS AFTER THE EXPIRATION OF THIS AGREEMENT

(4) Owner understands and agrees to pay the commission referred to in paragraph 3, if this property is sold or transferred or is the subject of a contract of sale within ____ months after the expiration date of this agreement involving a person with whom the Agent or a Cooperating Broker negotiated or to whom the property was offered, quoted or shown by Agent or any Cooperating Broker during the period of this listing agreement. Owner will not, however, be obligated to pay such commission if Owner enters into a valid Exclusive Listing Agreement with another licensed real estate broker after the expiration of this agreement.

WHO MAY NEGOTIATE FOR OWNER

(5) Owner elects to have all offers submitted through Agent ____ or Cooperating Agent ____.

SUBMISSION OF LISTING TO MULTIPLE LISTING SERVICE

(6) Both Owner and Agent agree that the Agent immediately is to submit this listing agreement to the Westchester Multiple Listing Service, Inc.

(WMLS) for dissemination to its Participants. No provision of this agreement is intended to nor shall be understood to establish or imply any contractual relationship between the Owner and the WMLS, nor has the WMLS in any way participated in any of the terms of this agreement, including the commission to be paid. Owner acknowledges that the Agent's ability to submit this listing to the WMLS, or to maintain such listing amongst those included in any compilation of listing information published by the WMLS, is subject to Agent's continued status as a member in good standing of the Westchester County Board of Realtors, Inc., and Agent's status as a Participant in good standing of WMLS.

FAIR HOUSING

(7) Agent and Owner agree to comply fully with local, state and federal fair housing laws against discrimination on the basis of race, color, religion, sex, national origin, handicap, age, marital status and/or familial status, children or other prohibited factors.

OTHER SERVICES

(8) Owner acknowledges that Agent has fully explained to Owner the services and marketing activities which Agent has agreed to provide.

REQUIREMENTS FOR PUBLICATION IN WMLS COMPILATION

(9) This listing agreement is not acceptable for publication by WMLS unless and until the Owner has duly signed this agreement and an acknowledgment reflecting receipt of the definitions of"Exclusive Right to Sell" and "Exclusive Agency" required by the New York State Department of State—Division of Licensing Services.

RENTAL OF PROPERTY

(10) Should the Owner desire to rent the property during the period of this agreement, Agent is hereby granted the sole and exclusive agency to rent the property, exclusive "For Rent" sign privilege and the Owner agrees to pay Agent a rental commission of ____. The applicable commission for the lease term is due and will be paid upon the execution of the lease ____ upon the date of occupancy ____. The commission for each and any subsequent renewal thereof, is due and will be paid upon the commencement of each renewal term.

TERMINATION

(11) Owner understands that if Owner terminates the Agent's authority prior to the expiration of its term, Agent shall retain its contract rights (including but not limited to recovery of its commission, advertising expenses and/or any other damages) incurred by reason of an early termination of this agreement.

ADDITIONAL POINTS

(12) Additional Points, of Agreement, if any:

IN-HOUSE SALES

(13) If the Broker has an agency relationship with the buyer ("buyer's broker"), and that buyer expresses interest in property owned by a seller who also has an agency relationship with the Broker ("seller's broker"), a conflict has arisen.

The Broker shall immediately advise both the buyer client and the seller client of the pertinent facts including the fact that a dual agency situation has arisen, and that the following options are available:

(a) The Broker and buyer could dissolve their Agency relationship. The buyer may then seek to retain another broker, and/or an attorney, or may represent himself. This would release the buyer from any Broker employment contract which was entered into with the Broker. Broker may continue to act as agent for the seller.

(b) The Broker and the seller could dissolve their Agency relationship. The seller may then seek to retain another broker, and/or an attorney, or may represent himself. This would release the seller from any listing agreement which was entered into with Broker. The Broker may continue to act as Agent for the buyer.

(c) With fully informed consent, the buyer and seller may elect to continue with the brokerage firm serving as a consensual dual agent, which is the exception to the general rule that agents serve one principal. As a dual agent, the firm and its licensee agents have a duty of fairness to both principals. By mutual agreement the buyer and seller may identify who will negotiate for each principal. For example: (a) the licensee who signed the buyer as a principal of the brokerage firm may negotiate on behalf of the buyer principal and (b) the licensee who signed the seller as a principal of the firm may negotiate on behalf of the seller principal.

In either case, the brokerage commission will be paid by the seller in accordance with the listing agreement with the seller, unless different arrangements have been negotiated.

As a dual agent, the firm and its agents cannot furnish undivided loyalty to either party.

As a dual agent, the firm and its licensee agents have a duty not to disclose confidential information given by one principal to the other principal, such as the price one is willing to pay or accept. Such information may already be known to the firm and its agents. If the information is of such a nature that the agent cannot fairly give advice without disclosing it, the agent cannot properly continue to act as an agent.

The buyer, seller and broker shall memorialize the option of their mutual choice by executing a statutory disclosure notice. If there is no mutual agreement, the proposed transaction between buyer and seller shall not be pursued.

ALL MODIFICATIONS TO BE MADE IN WRITING

(14) Owner and Agent agree that no change, amendment, modification or termination of this Agreement shall be binding on any party unless the same shall be in writing and signed by the parties.*

By: _____   _____
          Owner   Date

By: _____   _____
          Owner   Date

AGENT:

By: _____   _____
      Authorized Representative   Date

_____

*   Source: Westchester County Board of Realtors, Inc.

APPENDIX 6:
SAMPLE EXCLUSIVE RIGHT TO SELL AGREEMENT

EXCLUSIVE RIGHT TO SELL AGREEMENT

THIS AGREEMENT is effective _____, 20____, and confirms that _____
(Owner) has appointed _____ to act as Agent for the sale of property known as _____ in the State of New York.

In return for the Agent's agreement to use Agent's best efforts to sell the above property, the Owner agrees to grant the Agent an exclusive right to sell this property under the following terms and conditions:

PERIOD OF AGREEMENT

(1) This agreement shall be effective from the above date and shall expire at midnight on _____, 20____.

PRICE AT WHICH PROPERTY WILL BE OFFERED AND AUTHORITY

(2) The property will be offered for sale at a list price of _____ and shall be sold, subject to negotiation, at such price and upon such terms to which Owner may agree. The word Owner refers to each and all parties who have ownership interest in the property and the undersigned represents they are the sole and exclusive owners and are fully authorized to enter into this agreement.

COMMISSION TO BE PAID AGENT

(3) The Agent shall be entitled to and Owner shall pay to Agent one commission of ____ of the selling price. Both the Owner and Agent acknowledge that the above commission rate was not suggested nor influenced by anyone other than the parties to this Agreement. Owner hereby authorizes Agent to make an offer of cooperation to any other licensed real estate broker with whom Agent wishes to cooperate. Any commission due for a sale brought about by a Sub-Agent (another broker who is authorized by Agent to assist in the sale of Owner's property) or to an authorized Buyer's Agent shall be paid by the Agent from the commission received by the Agent pursuant to this Paragraph.

The commission offered by Agent to Sub-Agents shall be ____ of the gross selling price. The commission offered by Agent to Buyer's Agent shall be ____ of the gross selling price.

In the event that Owner authorizes Agent to compensate a Buyer's Agent, Owner acknowledges Owner's understanding that such Buyer's Agent is not representing Owner as Sub-Agent and that the Buyer's Agent will be representing only the interests of the prospective purchaser.

OWNER'S OBLIGATIONS AFTER THE EXPIRATION OF THIS AGREEMENT

(4) Owner understands and agrees to pay the commission referred to in paragraph 3, if this property is sold or transferred or is the subject of a contract of sale within ____ months after the expiration date of this agreement involving a person with whom the Agent or a Cooperating Broker negotiated or to whom the property was offered, quoted or shown by Agent or any Cooperating Broker during the period of this listing agreement. Owner will not, however, be obligated to pay such commission if Owner enters into a valid Exclusive Listing Agreement with another licensed real estate broker after the expiration of this agreement.

WHO MAY NEGOTIATE FOR OWNER

(5) Owner agrees to direct all inquiries to the Agent. Owner elects to have all offers submitted through Agent ____ or Cooperating Agent ____.

SUBMISSION OF LISTING TO MULTIPLE LISTING SERVICE

(6) Both Owner and Agent agree that the Agent immediately is to submit this listing agreement to the Westchester Multiple Listing Service, Inc. (WMLS) for dissemination to its Participants. No provision of this agreement is intended to nor shall be understood to establish or imply any contractual relationship between the Owner and the WMLS, nor has the WMLS in any way participated in any of the terms of this agreement, including the commission to be paid. Owner acknowledges that the Agent's ability to submit this listing to the WMLS, or to maintain such listing amongst those included in any compilation of listing information published by the WMLS, is subject to Agent's continued status as a member in good standing of the Westchester County Board of Realtors, Inc., and Agent's status as a Participant in good standing of WMLS.

FAIR HOUSING

(7) Agent and Owner agree to comply fully with local, state and federal fair housing laws against discrimination on the basis of race, color, religion, sex, national origin, handicap, age, marital status and/or familial status, children or other prohibited factors.

AUTHORIZATION FOR "FOR SALE" SIGN AND OTHER SERVICES

(8) Agent is ____ is not ____ authorized to place a "For Sale" sign on the property. Owner acknowledges that the Agent has fully explained to Owner the services and marketing activities which Agent has agreed to provide.

REQUIREMENTS FOR PUBLICATION IN WMLS COMPILATION

(9) This listing agreement is not acceptable for publication by WMLS unless and until the Owner has duly signed this agreement and an acknowledgment reflecting receipt of the definitions of "Exclusive Right to Sell" and "Exclusive Agency" required by the New York State Department of State—Division of Licensing Services.

RENTAL OF PROPERTY

(10) Should the Owner desire to rent the property during the period of this agreement, Agent is hereby granted the sole and exclusive right to

rent the property, exclusive "For Rent" sign privilege and the Owner agrees to pay Agent a rental commission of ____. The applicable commission for the lease term is due and will be paid upon the execution of the lease ____ upon the date of occupancy ____. The commission for each and any subsequent renewal thereof, is due and will be paid upon the commencement of each renewal term.

TERMINATION

(11) Owner understands that if Owner terminates the Agent's authority prior to the expiration of its term, Agent shall retain its contract rights (including but not limited to recovery of its commission, advertising expenses and/or any other damages) incurred by reason of an early termination of this agreement.

ADDITIONAL POINTS

(12) Additional Points, of Agreement, if any:

IN-HOUSE SALES

(13) If the Broker has an agency relationship with the buyer ("buyer's broker"), and that buyer expresses interest in property owned by a seller who also has an agency relationship with the Broker ("seller's broker"), a conflict has arisen.

The Broker shall immediately advise both the buyer client and the seller client of the pertinent facts including the fact that a dual agency situation has arisen, and that the following options are available:

(a) The Broker and buyer could dissolve their Agency relationship. The buyer may then seek to retain another broker, and/or an attorney, or may represent himself. This would release the buyer from any Broker employment contract which was entered into with the Broker. Broker may continue to act as agent for the seller.

(b) The Broker and the seller could dissolve their Agency relationship. The seller may then seek to retain another broker, and/or an attorney, or may represent himself. This would release the seller from any listing agreement which was entered into with Broker. The Broker may continue to act as Agent for the buyer.

(c) With fully informed consent, the buyer and seller may elect to continue with the brokerage firm serving as a consensual dual agent, which is the exception to the general rule that agents serve one principal. As a dual agent, the firm and its licensee agents have a duty of fairness to both principals. By mutual agreement the buyer and seller may identify who will negotiate for each principal. For example: (a) the licensee who signed the buyer as a principal of the brokerage firm may negotiate on behalf of the buyer principal and (b) the licensee who signed the seller as a principal of the firm may negotiate on behalf of the seller principal.

In either case, the brokerage commission will be paid by the seller in accordance with the listing agreement with the seller, unless different arrangements have been negotiated.

As a dual agent, the firm and its agents cannot furnish undivided loyalty to either party.

As a dual agent, the firm and its licensee agents have a duty not to disclose confidential information given by one principal to the other principal, such as the price one is willing to pay or accept. Such information may already be known to the firm and its agents. If the information is of such a nature that the agent cannot fairly give advice without disclosing it, the agent cannot properly continue to act as an agent.

The buyer, seller and broker shall memorialize the option of their mutual choice by executing a statutory disclosure notice. If there is no mutual agreement, the proposed transaction between buyer and seller shall not be pursued.

ALL MODIFICATIONS TO BE MADE IN WRITING

(14) Owner and Agent agree that no change, amendment, modification or termination of this Agreement shall be binding on any party unless the same shall be in writing and signed by the parties.*

By: _____   _____
                 Owner   Date

By: _____   _____
                 Owner   Date

AGENT:

By: _____   _____
        Authorized Representative   Date

---

*   Source: Westchester County Board of Realtors, Inc.

APPENDIX 7:
MORTGAGE PAYMENT ESTIMATION CHART

INTEREST RATE (%)	10 YEARS	15 YEARS	20 YEARS	25 YEARS	30 YEARS
5.00	$10.61	$7.91	$ 6.60	$5.85	$ 5.37
5.25	$10.73	$8.04	$6.74	$5.99	$5.52
5.50	$10.85	$8.17	$6.88	$6.14	$5.68
5.75	$10.98	$8.30	$7.02	$6.29	$5.84
6.00	$11.10	$8.44	$7.16	$6.44	$6.00
6.25	$11.23	$8.57	$7.31	$6.60	$6.16
6.50	$11.35	$8.71	$7.46	$6.75	$6.32
6.75	$11.48	$8.85	$7.60	$6.91	$6.49
7.00	$11.61	$8.99	$7.75	$7.07	$6.65
7.25	$11.74	$9.13	$7.90	$7.23	$6.82
7.50	$11.87	$9.27	$8.06	$7.39	$6.99
7.75	$12.00	$9.41	$8.21	$7.55	$7.16
8.00	$12.13	$9.56	$8.36	$7.72	$7.34
8.25	$12.27	$9.70	$8.52	$7.88	$7.51
8.50	$12.40	$9.85	$8.68	$8.05	$7.69
8.75	$12.53	$9.99	$8.84	$8.22	$7.87
9.00	$12.67	$10.14	$9.00	$8.39	$8.05

9.25	$12.80	$10.29	$9.16	$8.56	$8.23
9.50	$12.94	$10.44	$9.32	$8.74	$8.41
9.75	$13.08	$10.59	$9.49	$8.91	$8.59
10.00	$13.22	$10.75	$9.65	$9.09	$8.78

DIRECTIONS FOR ESTIMATING MONTHLY MORTGAGE PAYMENTS:

Select the interest rate and term for the mortgage loan you are considering to ascertain your monthly payment per $1000 of loan principal. For example, if you are considering a mortgage loan in the amount of $50,000 which carries an interest rate of 7.50% for a term of 30 years, multiply the indicated amount of $6.99 by 50 ($50,000/100). Thus, $349.50 is the estimated monthly payment not including taxes, insurance or miscellaneous closing costs.

APPENDIX 8:
CLOSING COST ESTIMATOR

BUYERS ESTIMATED CLOSING COSTS

ITEM	ESTIMATED AMOUNT	ACTUAL AMOUNT
(1) Application Fee: Charged by Lender	May range from $100–$300	$_____
(2) Appraisal Fee	Approximately $250	$_____
(3) Credit Report	Approximately $50	$_____
(4) Escrow Fees (Insurance): Amounts paid to lender for insurance	Generally includes advance payments of homeowner's insurance (2 months); and flood and PMI insurance, when required (2 months)	$_____
(5) Escrow Fees (Taxes): Amounts paid to lender for property and school taxes	Generally includes advance (3 months)	$_____
(6) Flood Certification Fee: Required by lender to verify flood zone status of property	Approximately $15.	$_____
(7) Flood Insurance	Varies depending on flood zone, Generally $500–$1000 per year	$_____
(8) Funding Fee	a percentage of the loan amount charged on VA loans instead of PMI	$_____
(9) Home Inspection	Approximately $300–$500	$_____
(10) Homeowner's Insurance	Varies, generally .0025 of purchase price per year	$_____

(11) Buyer's Legal Fees	Legal fees vary depending on attorney and location, but generally range from $750–$1,000	$_____
(12) Lender's Legal Fee: For review of documents	Ranges from $150–$250, where applicable	$_____
(13) Mortgage Tax	Generally 0.75% of mortgage amount, where applicable	$_____
(14) Points: Amount paid to lender to "buydown" interest rate on mortgage	Usually ranges from 0 to 3 points	$_____
(15) Prepaid Interest	Interest on mortgage payable to lender from date of closing to end of 1st month	$_____
(16) Private Mortgage Insurance: PMI is required if mortgage is more than 80% of purchase price	Generally .004 of mortgage amount	$_____
(17) Recording Fees	Approximately $50–$75	$_____

APPENDIX 9:
SELECTED PROVISIONS OF THE NATIONAL MANUFACTURED HOUSING CONSTRUCTION AND SAFETY STANDARDS ACT (42 U.S.C. §5401 ET SEQ)

42 U.S.C. § 5401. Congressional declaration of purposes

The Congress declares that the purposes of this chapter are to reduce the number of personal injuries and deaths and the amount of insurance costs and property damage resulting from manufactured home accidents and to improve the quality and durability of manufactured homes. Therefore, the Congress determines that it is necessary to establish Federal construction and safety standards for manufactured homes and to authorize manufactured home safety research and development.

42 U.S.C. § 5402. Definitions

As used in this chapter, the term—

(1) "manufactured home construction" means all activities relating to the assembly and manufacture of a manufactured home including but not limited to those relating to durability, quality, and safety;

(2) "dealer" means any person engaged in the sale, leasing, or distribution of new manufactured homes primarily to persons who in good faith purchase or lease a manufactured home for purposes other than resale;

(3) "defect" includes any defect in the performance, construction, components, or material of a manufactured home that renders the home or any part thereof not fit for the ordinary use for which it was intended;

(4) "distributor" means any person engaged in the sale and distribution of manufactured homes for resale;

(5) "manufacturer" means any person engaged in manufacturing or assembling manufactured homes, including any person engaged in importing manufactured homes for resale;

(6) "manufactured home" means a structure, transportable in one or more sections, which, in the traveling mode, is eight body feet or more in width or forty body feet or more in length, or, when erected on site, is three hundred twenty or more square feet, and which is built on a permanent chassis and designed to be used as a dwelling with or without a permanent foundation when connected to the required utilities, and includes the plumbing, heating, air-conditioning, and electrical systems contained therein; except that such term shall include any structure which meets all the requirements of this paragraph except the size requirements and with respect to which the manufacturer voluntarily files a certification required by the Secretary and complies with the standards established under this chapter; and except that such term shall not include any self-propelled recreational vehicle;

(7) "Federal manufactured home construction and safety standard" means a reasonable standard for the construction, design, and performance of a manufactured home which meets the needs of the public including the need for quality, durability, and safety;

(8) "manufactured home safety" means the performance of a manufactured home in such a manner that the public is protected against any unreasonable risk of the occurrence of accidents due to the design or construction of such manufactured home, or any unreasonable risk of death or injury to the user or to the public if such accidents do occur;

(9) "imminent safety hazard" means an imminent and unreasonable risk of death or severe personal injury;

(10) "purchaser" means the first person purchasing a manufactured home in good faith for purposes other than resale;

(11) "Secretary" means the Secretary of Housing and Urban Development;

(12) "State" includes each of the several States, the District of Columbia, the Commonwealth of Puerto Rico, Guam, the Virgin Islands, the Canal Zone, and American Samoa; and

(13) "United States district courts" means the Federal district courts of the United States and the United States courts of the Commonwealth of Puerto Rico, Guam, the Virgin Islands, the Canal Zone, and American Samoa.

42 U.S.C. § 5409. Prohibited acts; exemptions

(a) No person shall—

(1) make use of any means of transportation or communication affecting interstate or foreign commerce or the mails to manufacture for sale, lease, sell, offer for sale or lease, or introduce or deliver, or import into the United States, any manufactured home which is manufactured on or after the effective date of any applicable Federal manufactured home construction and safety standard under this chapter and which does not comply with such standard, except as provided in subsection (b) of this section, where such manufacture, lease, sale, offer for sale or lease, introduction, delivery, or importation affects commerce;

(2) fail or refuse to permit access to or copying of records, or fail to make reports or provide information, or fail or refuse to permit entry or inspection, as required under section 5413 of this title;

(3) fail to furnish notification of any defect as required by

(4) fail to issue a certification required by section 5415 of this title, or issue a certification to the effect that a manufactured home conforms to all applicable Federal manufactured home construction and safety standards, if such person in the exercise of due care has reason to know that such certification is false or misleading in a material respect;

(5) fail to comply with a final order issued by the Secretary

(6) issue a certification pursuant to subsection (h) of section 5403 of this title, if such person in the exercise of due care has reason to know that such certification is false or misleading in a material respect.

(b)(1) Paragraph (1) of subsection (a) of this section shall not apply to the sale, the offer for sale, or the introduction or delivery for introduction in interstate commerce of any manufactured home after the first purchase of it in good faith for purposes other than resale.

(2) For purposes of section 5410 of this title, paragraph (1) of subsection (a) of this section shall not apply to any person who establishes that he did not have reason to know in the exercise of due care that such manufactured home is not in conformity with applicable Federal manufactured home construction and safety standards, or to any person who, prior to such first purchase, holds a certificate issued by the manufacturer or importer of such manufactured home to the effect that such manufactured home conforms to all applicable Federal manufactured home construction and safety standards, unless such person knows that such manufactured home does not so conform.

(3) A manufactured home offered for importation in violation of paragraph (1) of subsection (a) of this section shall be refused admission into the United States under joint regulations issued by the Secretary of the Treasury and the Secretary, except that the Secretary of the Treasury and the Secretary may, by such regulations, provide for authorizing the importation of such manufactured home into the United States upon such terms and conditions (including the furnishing of a bond) as may appear to them appropriate to insure that any such manufactured home will be brought into conformity with any applicable Federal manufactured home construction or safety standard prescribed under this chapter, or will be exported from, or forfeited to, the United States.

(4) The Secretary of the Treasury and the Secretary may, by joint regulations, permit the importation of any manufactured home after the first purchase of it in good faith for purposes other than resale.

(5) Paragraph (1) of subsection (a) of this section shall not apply in the case of a manufactured home intended solely for export, and so labeled or tagged on the manufactured home itself and on the outside of the container, if any, in which it is to be exported.

(c) Compliance with any Federal manufactured home construction or safety standard issued under this chapter does not exempt any person from any liability under common law.

42 U.S.C. § 5410. Civil and criminal penalties

(a) Whoever violates any provision of section 5409 of this title, or any regulation or final order issued thereunder, shall be liable to the United States for a civil penalty of not to exceed $1,000 for each such violation. Each violation of a provision of section 5409 of this title, or any regulation or order issued the manufactured home or with respect to each failure or refusal to allow or perform an act required thereby, except that the maximum civil penalty may not exceed $1,000,000 for any related series of violations occurring within one year from the date of the first violation.

(b) An individual or a director, officer, or agent of a corporation who knowingly and willfully violates section 5409 of this title in a manner which threatens the health or safety of any purchaser shall be fined not more than $1,000 or imprisoned not more than one year, or both.

42 U.S.C. § 5412. Noncompliance with standards or defective nature of manufactured home; administrative or judicial determination; repurchase by manufacturer or repair by distributor or dealer; reimbursement of expenses, etc., by manufacturer; injunctive relief against manufacturer for failure to comply; jurisdiction and venue; damages; period of limitation

(a) If the Secretary or a court of appropriate jurisdiction determines that any manufactured home does not conform to applicable Federal manufactured home construction and safety standards, or that it contains a defect which constitutes an imminent safety hazard, after the sale of such manufactured home by a manufacturer to a distributor or a dealer and prior to the sale of such manufactured home by such distributor or dealer to a purchaser—

(1) the manufacturer shall immediately repurchase such manufactured home from such distributor or dealer at the price paid by such distributor or dealer, plus all transportation charges involved and a reasonable reimbursement of not less than 1 per centum per month of such price paid prorated from the date of receipt by certified mail of notice of such nonconformance to the date

(2) the manufacturer, at his own expense, shall immediately furnish the purchasing distributor or dealer the required conforming part or parts or equipment for installation by the distributor or dealer on or in such manufactured home, and for the installation involved the manufacturer shall reimburse such distributor or dealer for the reasonable value of such installation plus a reasonable reimbursement of not less than 1 per centum per month of the manufacturer's or distributor's selling price prorated from the date of receipt by certified mail of notice of such nonconformance to the date such vehicle is brought into conformance with applicable Federal standards, so long as the distributor or dealer proceeds with reasonable diligence with the installation after the required part or equipment is received. The value of such reasonable reimbursements as specified in paragraphs (1) and (2) of this subsection shall be fixed by mutual agreement of the parties, or, failing such agreement, by the court pursuant to the provisions of subsection (b) of this section.

(b) If any manufacturer fails to comply with the requirements of subsection (a) of this section, then the distributor or dealer, as the case may be, to whom such manufactured home has been sold may bring an action seeking a court injunction compelling compliance with such requirements on the part of such manufacturer. Such action may be brought in any district court in the United States in the district in which such manufacturer resides, or is found, or has an agent, without regard to the amount in controversy, and the person bringing the action shall also be entitled to recover any damage sustained by him, as well as all court costs plus reasonable attorneys' fees. Any action brought pursuant to this section shall be forever barred unless commenced within three years after the cause of action shall have accrued.

42 U.S.C. § 5415. Certification by manufacturer of conformity of manufactured home with standards; form and placement of certification

Every manufacturer of manufactured homes shall furnish to the distributor or dealer at the time of delivery of each such manufactured home produced by such manufacturer certification that such manufactured home conforms to all applicable Federal construction and safety standards. Such certification shall be in the form of a label or tag permanently affixed to each such manufactured home.

42 U.S.C. § 5416. Consumer's manual; contents

The Secretary shall develop guidelines for a consumer's manual to be provided to manufactured home purchasers by the manufacturer. These manuals should identify and explain the purchasers' responsibilities for operation, maintenance, and repair of their manufactured homes.

APPENDIX 10:
DIRECTORY OF STATE ADMINISTRATIVE AGENCIES ADMINISTERING THE HUD MANUFACTURED HOUSING PROGRAM

STATE	ORGANIZATION	ADDRESS	TELEPHONE	FAX
ALABAMA	Manufactured Housing Commission	350 S. Decatur St. Montgomery, AL 36104	(334) 242-4036	(334) 240-3178
ARIZONA	Dept. of Building and Fire Safety Office of Manufactured Housing	99 East Virginia Suite 100 Phoenix, AZ 85004	(602) 255-4072	(602) 255-4962

STATE	ORGANIZATION	ADDRESS	TELEPHONE	FAX
ARKANSAS	Arkansas Manufactured Home Commission	523 S. Louisiana St. Suite 500 Lafayette Bldg, Little Rock, AR 72201	(501) 324-9032	(501) 324-9034
CALIFORNIA	Dept. of Housing and Community Development, Division of Codes and Standards Manufactured Housing Section	1800 3rd St. Suite 260 Sacramento, CA 95814	(916) 445-3338	(916) 327-4712
COLORADO	Housing Division Dept. of Local Affairs	1313 Sherman St. Suite 518 Denver, CO 80203	(303) 866-2033	(303) 866-4077
FLORIDA	Bureau of Mobile Homes and Recreational Vehicles Construction Division of Motor Vehicles	2900 Apalachee Pkwy. Room A-129 Tallahassee, FL 32399-0640	(850) 488-8600	(850) 488-7053
GEORGIA	Manufactured Housing Division State Fire Marshal's Office	#2 Martin Luther King Jr. Dr. #620 West Tower Atlanta, GA 30334	(404) 656-9498.	(404) 657-6971
IDAHO	Division of Building Safety Building Bureau	277 N. Sixth St. Suite 100 P. O. Box 83720 Boise, ID 83720-0060	(208) 334-3896	(208) 334-2683
INDIANA	Codes Enforcement Division Dept. of Fire and Building Services	402 W. Washington St. Room W-246 Indianapolis, IN 46204-2739	(317) 232-6422	(317) 232-0146

STATE	ORGANIZATION	ADDRESS	TELEPHONE	FAX
IOWA	Iowa State Building Code Bureau Dept. of Public Safety	621 East Second Street Des Moines, IA 50309-1831	(515) 281-5821	(515) 242-6299
KENTUCKY	Manufactured Housing Division Dept. of Housing, Building and Construction	1047 U.S. 127 South Suite #1 Frankfort, KY 40601-4337	(502) 564-3626	(502) 564-6799
LOUISIANA	Manufactured Housing Division State Fire Marshal's Office	5150 Florida Blvd. Baton Rouge, LA 70806	(225) 925-4911/ (800) 256-5452	(225) 925-3699
MAINE	Manufactured Housing Board Dept. of Professional and Financial Regulation	35 State Housing Station Augusta, ME 04333	(207) 624-8612	(207) 624-8637
MARYLAND	Dept. of Housing and Community Development Maryland Code Administration	100 Community Pl. Crownsville, MD 21032-2023	(410) 514-7213	(410) 987-8902
MICHIGAN	Manufactured Housing Division Corporation Securities and Land Development Bureau	P.O. Box 30222 Lansing, MI 48909	(517) 334-6203	(517) 334-6842
MINNESOTA	Department of Administration, Manufactured Structures Section Minnesota Building Codes and Standards Division	121 7th Place E. Suite 408 St. Paul, MN 55101-2181	(651) 296-4639	(651) 297-1973
MISSISSIPPI	Manufactured Housing Division Office of the State Fire Marshal	P.O. Box 22542 Jackson, MS 39225	(601) 354-6900	(601) 354-6899
MISSOURI	Dept. of Manufactured Housing and Recreational Vehicle and Modular Units Public Service Commission	301 W. High Street Jefferson City, MO 65101	(573) 751-7435	(573) 751-1847

STATE	ORGANIZATION	ADDRESS	TELEPHONE	FAX
NEBRASKA	Nebraska Public Service Commission Housing & Recreational Vehicle Department	300 The Atrium 1200 "N" Street P. O. Box 94927 Lincoln, NE 68509	(402) 471-0518	(402) 471-7709
NEVADA	Dept. of Business & Industry Manufactured Housing Division	2501 E. Sahara Ave. Suite 204 Las Vegas, NV 89104	(702) 486-4135	(702) 486-4309
NEW JERSEY	New Jersey Division of Codes & Standards Bureau of Code Services	P. O. Box 816 Trenton, NJ 08625-0816	(609) 530-8833	(609) 530-8357
NEW MEXICO	Manufactured Housing Division Regulation and Licensing Department	725 St. Michael's Drive Santa Fe, NM 87504	(505) 827-7070	(505) 827-7074
NEW YORK	New York Department of State Codes Division	41 State Street Room 1130 Albany, NY 12231	(518) 474-4073	(518) 486-4487
NORTH CAROLINA	Manufactured Building Division Dept. of Insurance	410 N. Boylan Avenue Raleigh, NC 27603	(919) 733-3901	(919) 715-9693
OREGON	Dept. of Consumer and Business Services Building Codes Division	P. O. Box 14470 Salem, OR 97309	(503) 378-5975	(503) 378-4101
PENNSYLVANIA	Manufactured Housing Division Community Development and Housing Office Department of Community Economy Development	314 Forum Building Harrisburg, PA 17120-0155	(717) 720-7413	(717) 783-4663

STATE	ORGANIZATION	ADDRESS	TELEPHONE	FAX
RHODE ISLAND	Building Code Commission Dept. of Administration	One Capitol Hill Providence, RI 02908-5859	(401) 222-3033	(401) 222-2599
SOUTH CAROLINA	South Carolina Dept. of Labor, Licensing and Regulation Real Estate & Building Code Professions	110 Centerview Drive Suite 102 Columbia, SC 29211-1329	(803) 896-4688	(803) 896-6038
SOUTH DAKOTA	Commercial Inspection and Regulation Division Dept. of Commerce and Regulations	118 W. Capitol Avenue Pierre, SD 57501-5070	(605) 773-3697	(605) 773-6631
TENNESSEE	Codes and Standards Division of Fire Prevention	500 James Robertson Pkwy Nashville, TN 37243-1160	(615) 741-7170	(615) 741-1583
TEXAS	Manufactured Housing Division Dept. of Housing and Community Affairs	507 Sabine Street 10th Floor Austin, TX 78701	1-800-500-7074	(512) 475-4760
UTAH	Division of Occupational and Professional Licensing, Department of Commerce	P. O. Box 146741 Salt Lake City, UT 84114-6764	(801) 530-6727	(801) 530-6511
VIRGINIA	Manufactured Housing Office Dept. of Housing and Community Development	Jackson Center 501 N. Second Street Richmond, VA 23219	(804) 371-7160	(804) 371-7092
WASHINGTON	Office of Manufactured Housing Dept. of Community Trade and Economic Development	906 Columbia Street SW Olympia, WA 98504-8300	(360) 586-1362	(360) 586-5880

STATE	ORGANIZATION	ADDRESS	TELEPHONE	FAX
WEST VIRGINIA	West Virginia Division of Labor	319 Building Three Capitol Complex Charleston, WV 25305	(304) 586-1362	(304) 558-3797
WISCONSIN	Department of Commerce Manufactured Homes Safety and Building Division	201 W. Washington Avenue P.O. Box 7332 Madison, WI 53707-7302	(608) 266-8577	(608) 267-0592

Source: United States Department of Housing and Urban Development

APPENDIX 11:
SELECTED PROVISIONS OF THE FAIR
HOUSING ACT (42 U.S.C. §3601 ET SEQ)

Sec. 3601. Declaration of policy

It is the policy of the United States to provide, within constitutional limitations, for fair housing throughout the United States.

Sec. 3602. Definitions

As used in this subchapter—

(a) "Secretary" means the Secretary of Housing and Urban Development.

(b) "Dwelling" means any building, structure, or portion thereof which is occupied as, or designed or intended for occupancy as, a residence by one or more families, and any vacant land which is offered for sale or lease for the construction or location thereon of any such building, structure, or portion thereof.

(c) "Family" includes a single individual.

(d) "Person" includes one or more individuals, corporations, partnerships, associations, labor organizations, legal representatives, mutual companies, joint-stock companies, trusts, unincorporated organizations, trustees, trustees in cases under title 11, receivers, and fiduciaries.

(e) "To rent" includes to lease, to sublease, to let and otherwise to grant for a consideration the right to occupy premises not owned by the occupant.

(f) "Discriminatory housing practice" means an act that is unlawful under section 3604, 3605, 3606, or 3617 of this title.

(g) "State" means any of the several States, the District of Columbia, the Commonwealth of Puerto Rico, or any of the territories and possessions of the United States.

(h) "Handicap" means, with respect to a person—

(1) a physical or mental impairment which substantially limits one or more of such person's major life activities,

(2) a record of having such an impairment, or

(3) being regarded as having such an impairment, but such term does not include current, illegal use of or addiction to a controlled substance (as defined in section 802 of title 21).

(i) "Aggrieved person" includes any person who—

(1) claims to have been injured by a discriminatory housing practice; or

(2) believes that such person will be injured by a discriminatory housing practice that is about to occur.

(j) "Complainant" means the person (including the Secretary) who files a complaint under section 3610 of this title.

(k) "Familial status" means one or more individuals (who have not attained the age of 18 years) being domiciled with—

(1) a parent or another person having legal custody of such individual or individuals; or

(2) the designee of such parent or other person having such custody, with the written permission of such parent or other person. The protections afforded against discrimination on the basis of familial status shall apply to any person who is pregnant or is in the process of securing legal custody of any individual who has not attained the age of 18 years.

(l) "Conciliation" means the attempted resolution of issues raised by a complaint, or by the investigation of such complaint, through informal negotiations involving the aggrieved person, the respondent, and the Secretary.

(m) "Conciliation agreement" means a written agreement setting forth the resolution of the issues in conciliation.

(n) "Respondent" means—

(1) the person or other entity accused in a complaint of an unfair housing practice; and

(2) any other person or entity identified in the course of investigation and notified as required with respect to respondents so identified under section 3610(a) of this title.

(o) "Prevailing party" has the same meaning as such term has in section 1988 of this title.

Sec. 3603. Effective dates of certain prohibitions

(a) Application to certain described dwellings Subject to the provisions of subsection (b) of this section and section 3607 of this title, the prohibitions against discrimination in the sale or rental of housing set forth in section 3604 of this title shall apply:

(1) Upon enactment of this subchapter, to—

(A) dwellings owned or operated by the Federal Government;

(B) dwellings provided in whole or in part with the aid of loans, advances, grants, or contributions made by the Federal Government, under agreements entered into after November 20, 1962, unless payment due thereon has been made in full prior to April 11, 1968;

(C) dwellings provided in whole or in part by loans insured, guaranteed, or otherwise secured by the credit of the Federal Government, under agreements entered into after November 20, 1962, unless payment thereon has been made in full prior to April 11, 1968: Provided, That nothing contained in subparagraphs (B) and (C) of this subsection shall be applicable to dwellings solely by virtue of the fact that they are subject to mortgages held by an FDIC or FSLIC institution; and (D) dwellings provided by the development or the redevelopment of real property purchased, rented, or otherwise obtained from a State or local public agency receiving Federal financial assistance for slum clearance or urban renewal with respect to such real property under loan or grant contracts entered into after November 20, 1962.

(2) After December 31, 1968, to all dwellings covered by paragraph (1) and to all other dwellings except as exempted by subsection (b) of this section.

(b) Exemptions Nothing in section 3604 of this title (other than subsection (c)) shall apply to—

(1) any single-family house sold or rented by an owner: Provided, That such private individual owner does not own more than three such single-family houses at any one time: Provided further, That in

the case of the sale of any such single-family house by a private individual owner not residing in such house at the time of such sale or who was not the most recent resident of such house prior to such sale, the exemption granted by this subsection shall apply only with respect to one such sale within any twenty-four month period: Provided further, That such bona fide private individual owner does not own any interest in, nor is there owned or reserved on his behalf, under any express or voluntary agreement, title to or any right to all or a portion of the proceeds from the sale or rental of, more than three such single-family houses at any one time: Provided further, That after December 31, 1969, the sale or rental of any such single-family house shall be excepted from the application of this subchapter only if such house is sold or rented (A) without the use in any manner of the sales or rental facilities or the sales or rental services of any real estate broker, agent, or salesman, or of such facilities or services of any person in the business of selling or renting dwellings, or of any employee or agent of any such broker, agent, salesman, or person and (B) without the publication, posting or mailing, after notice, of any advertisement or written notice in violation of section 3604(c) of this title; but nothing in this proviso shall prohibit the use of attorneys, escrow agents, abstractors, title companies, and other such professional assistance as necessary to perfect or transfer the title, or

(2) rooms or units in dwellings containing living quarters occupied or intended to be occupied by no more than four families living independently of each other, if the owner actually maintains and occupies one of such living quarters as his residence.

(c) Business of selling or renting dwellings defined For the purposes of subsection (b) of this section, a person shall be deemed to be in the business of selling or renting dwellings if—

(1) he has, within the preceding twelve months, participated as principal in three or more transactions involving the sale or rental of any dwelling or any interest therein, or

(2) he has, within the preceding twelve months, participated as agent, other than in the sale of his own personal residence in providing sales or rental facilities or sales or rental services in two or more transactions involving the sale or rental of any dwelling or any interest therein, or

(3) he is the owner of any dwelling designed or intended for occupancy by, or occupied by, five or more families.

Sec. 3604. Discrimination in the sale or rental of housing and other prohibited practices

As made applicable by section 3603 of this title and except as exempted by sections 3603(b) and 3607 of this title, it shall be unlawful—

(a) To refuse to sell or rent after the making of a bona fide offer, or to refuse to negotiate for the sale or rental of, or otherwise make unavailable or deny, a dwelling to any person because of race, color, religion, sex, familial status, or national origin.

(b) To discriminate against any person in the terms, conditions, or privileges of sale or rental of a dwelling, or in the provision of services or facilities in connection therewith, because of race, color, religion, sex, familial status, or national origin.

(c) To make, print, or publish, or cause to be made, printed, or published any notice, statement, or advertisement, with respect to the sale or rental of a dwelling that indicates any preference, limitation, or discrimination based on race, color, religion, sex, handicap, familial status, or national origin, or an intention to make any such preference, limitation, or discrimination.

(d) To represent to any person because of race, color, religion, sex, handicap, familial status, or national origin that any dwelling is not available for inspection, sale, or rental when such dwelling is in fact so available.

(e) For profit, to induce or attempt to induce any person to sell or rent any dwelling by representations regarding the entry or prospective entry into the neighborhood of a person or persons of a particular race, color, religion, sex, handicap, familial status, or national origin.

(f) (1) To discriminate in the sale or rental, or to otherwise make unavailable or deny, a dwelling to any buyer or renter because of a handicap of—

(A) that buyer or renter,

(B) a person residing in or intending to reside in that dwelling after it is so sold, rented, or made available; or

(C) any person associated with that buyer or renter.

(f)(2) To discriminate against any person in the terms, conditions, or privileges of sale or rental of a dwelling, or in the provision of services or facilities in connection with such dwelling, because of a handicap of—

(A) that person; or

(B) a person residing in or intending to reside in that dwelling after it is so sold, rented, or made available; or

(C) any person associated with that person.

(f)(3) For purposes of this subsection, discrimination includes—

(A) a refusal to permit, at the expense of the handicapped person, reasonable modifications of existing premises occupied or to be occupied by such person if such modifications may be necessary to afford such person full enjoyment of the premises except that, in the case of a rental, the landlord may where it is reasonable to do so condition permission for a modification on the renter agreeing to restore the interior of the premises to the condition that existed before the modification, reasonable wear and tear excepted.

(B) a refusal to make reasonable accommodations in rules, policies, practices, or services, when such accommodations may be necessary to afford such person equal opportunity to use and enjoy a dwelling; or

(C) in connection with the design and construction of covered multifamily dwellings for first occupancy after the date that is 30 months after September 13, 1988, a failure to design and construct those dwellings in such a manner that—

(i) the public use and common use portions of such dwellings are readily accessible to and usable by handicapped persons;

(ii) all the doors designed to allow passage into and within all premises within such dwellings are sufficiently wide to allow passage by handicapped persons in wheelchairs; and

(iii) all premises within such dwellings contain the following features of adaptive design:

(I) an accessible route into and through the dwelling;

(II) light switches, electrical outlets, thermostats, and other environmental controls in accessible locations;

(III) reinforcements in bathroom walls to allow later installation of grab bars; and

(IV) usable kitchens and bathrooms such that an individual in a wheelchair can maneuver about the space.

(f)(4) Compliance with the appropriate requirements of the American National Standard for buildings and facilities providing accessibility and usability for physically handicapped people (commonly cited as

"ANSI A117.1") suffices to satisfy the requirements of paragraph (3)(C)(iii).

(f)(5)(A) If a State or unit of general local government has incorporated into its laws the requirements set forth in paragraph (3)(C), compliance with such laws shall be deemed to satisfy the requirements of that paragraph.

(B) A State or unit of general local government may review and approve newly constructed covered multifamily dwellings for the purpose of making determinations as to whether the design and construction requirements of paragraph (3)(C) are met.

(C) The Secretary shall encourage, but may not require, States and units of local government to include in their existing procedures for the review and approval of newly constructed covered multifamily dwellings, determinations as to whether the design and construction of such dwellings are consistent with paragraph (3)(C), and shall provide technical assistance to States and units of local government and other persons to implement the requirements of paragraph (3)(C).

(D) Nothing in this subchapter shall be construed to require the Secretary to review or approve the plans, designs or construction of all covered multifamily dwellings, to determine whether the design and construction of such dwellings are consistent with the requirements of paragraph 3(C).

(f)(6)(A) Nothing in paragraph (5) shall be construed to affect the authority and responsibility of the Secretary or a State or local public agency certified pursuant to section 3610(f)(3) of this title to receive and process complaints or otherwise engage in enforcement activities under this subchapter.

(B) Determinations by a State or a unit of general local government under paragraphs (5)(A) and (B) shall not be conclusive in enforcement proceedings under this subchapter.

(f)(7) As used in this subsection, the term "covered multifamily dwellings" means—

(A) buildings consisting of 4 or more units if such buildings have one or more elevators; and

(B) ground floor units in other buildings consisting of 4 or more units.

(f)(8) Nothing in this subchapter shall be construed to invalidate or limit any law of a State or political subdivision of a State, or other jurisdiction in which this subchapter shall be effective, that requires dwellings to be designed and constructed in a manner that affords handicapped persons greater access than is required by this subchapter.

(f)(9) Nothing in this subsection requires that a dwelling be made available to an individual whose tenancy would constitute a direct threat to the health or safety of other individuals or whose tenancy would result in substantial physical damage to the property of others.

Sec. 3605. Discrimination in residential real estate-related transactions

(a) In general

It shall be unlawful for any person or other entity whose business includes engaging in residential real estate-related transactions to discriminate against any person in making available such a transaction, or in the terms or conditions of such a transaction, because of race, color, religion, sex, handicap, familial status, or national origin.

(b) "Residential real estate-related transaction" defined As used in this section, the term "residential real estate-related transaction" means any of the following:

(1) The making or purchasing of loans or providing other financial assistance—

(A) for purchasing, constructing, improving, repairing, or maintaining a dwelling; or

(B) secured by residential real estate.

(2) The selling, brokering, or appraising of residential real property.

(c) Appraisal exemption

Nothing in this subchapter prohibits a person engaged in the business of furnishing appraisals of real property to take into consideration factors other than race, color, religion, national origin, sex, handicap, or familial status.

Sec. 3606. Discrimination in the provision of brokerage services

After December 31, 1968, it shall be unlawful to deny any person access to or membership or participation in any multiple-listing service, real estate brokers' organization or other service, organization, or facility relating to the business of selling or renting dwellings, or to discriminate against him in the terms or conditions of such access, membership, or participation, on account of race, color, religion, sex, handicap, familial status, or national origin.

Sec. 3607. Religious organization or private club exemption

(a) Nothing in this subchapter shall prohibit a religious organization, association, or society, or any nonprofit institution or organization operated, supervised or controlled by or in conjunction with a religious organization, association, or society, from limiting the sale, rental or occupancy of dwellings which it owns or operates for other than a commercial purpose to persons of the same religion, or from giving preference to such persons, unless membership in such religion is restricted on account of race, color, or national origin. Nor shall anything in this subchapter prohibit a private club not in fact open to the public, which as an incident to its primary purpose or purposes provides lodgings which it owns or operates for other than a commercial purpose, from limiting the rental or occupancy of such lodgings to its members or from giving preference to its members.

(b)(1) Nothing in this subchapter limits the applicability of any reasonable local, State, or Federal restrictions regarding the maximum number of occupants permitted to occupy a dwelling. Nor does any provision in this subchapter regarding familial status apply with respect to housing for older persons.

(2) As used in this section, "housing for older persons" means housing—

(A) provided under any State or Federal program that the Secretary determines is specifically designed and operated to assist elderly persons (as defined in the State or Federal program); or

(B) intended for, and solely occupied by, persons 62 years of age or older; or

(C) intended and operated for occupancy by persons 55 years of age or older, and—

(i) at least 80 percent of the occupied units are occupied by at least one person who is 55 years of age or older;

(ii) the housing facility or community publishes and adheres to policies and procedures that demonstrate the intent required under this subparagraph; and

(iii) the housing facility or community complies with rules issued by the Secretary for verification of occupancy, which shall—

(I) provide for verification by reliable surveys and affidavits; and

(II) include examples of the types of policies and procedures relevant to a determination of compliance with the requirement of clause (ii). Such surveys and affidavits shall be admissible in administrative and judicial proceedings for the purposes of such verification.

(3) Housing shall not fail to meet the requirements for housing for older persons by reason of:

(A) persons residing in such housing as of September 13, 1988, who do not meet the age requirements of subsections [1] (2) (B) or (C): Provided, That new occupants of such housing meet the age requirements of subsections [1] (2)(B) or (C); or

(B) unoccupied units: Provided, That such units are reserved for occupancy by persons who meet the age requirements of subsections [1] (2)(B) or (C).

(4) Nothing in this subchapter prohibits conduct against a person because such person has been convicted by any court of competent jurisdiction of the illegal manufacture or distribution of a controlled substance as defined in section 802 of title 21.

(5)(A) A person shall not be held personally liable for monetary damages for a violation of this subchapter if such person reasonably relied, in good faith, on the application of the exemption under this subsection relating to housing for older persons.

(B) For the purposes of this paragraph, a person may only show good faith reliance on the application of the exemption by showing that—

(i) such person has no actual knowledge that the facility or community is not, or will not be, eligible for such exemption; and

(ii) the facility or community has stated formally, in writing, that the facility or community complies with the requirements for such exemption.

Sec. 3608. Administration

(a) Authority and responsibility

The authority and responsibility for administering this Act shall be in the Secretary of Housing and Urban Development.

Sec. 3609.

(a) Complaints and answers

(1)(A)(i) An aggrieved person may, not later than one year after an alleged discriminatory housing practice has occurred or terminated, file a complaint with the Secretary alleging such discriminatory housing practice. The Secretary, on the Secretary's own initiative, may also file such a complaint.

(ii) Such complaints shall be in writing and shall contain such information and be in such form as the Secretary requires.

(iii) The Secretary may also investigate housing practices to determine whether a complaint should be brought under this section.

(B) Upon the filing of such a complaint—

(i) the Secretary shall serve notice upon the aggrieved person acknowledging such filing and advising the aggrieved person of the time limits and choice of forums provided under this subchapter;

(ii) the Secretary shall, not later than 10 days after such filing or the identification of an additional respondent under paragraph (2), serve on the respondent a notice identifying the alleged discriminatory housing practice and advising such respondent of the procedural rights and obligations of respondents under this subchapter, together with a copy of the original complaint;

(iii) each respondent may file, not later than 10 days after receipt of notice from the Secretary, an answer to such complaint; and

(iv) the Secretary shall make an investigation of the alleged discriminatory housing practice and complete such investigation within 100 days after the filing of the complaint (or, when the Secretary takes further action under subsection (f)(2) of this section with respect to a complaint, within 100 days after the commencement of such further action), unless it is impracticable to do so.

(C) If the Secretary is unable to complete the investigation within 100 days after the filing of the complaint (or, when the Secretary takes further action under subsection (f)(2) of this section with respect to a complaint, within 100 days after the commencement of such further action), the Secretary shall notify the complainant and respondent in writing of the reasons for not doing so.

(D) Complaints and answers shall be under oath or affirmation, and may be reasonably and fairly amended at any time.

(2)(A) A person who is not named as a respondent in a complaint, but who is identified as a respondent in the course of investigation, may be joined as an additional or substitute respondent upon written notice, under paragraph (1), to such person, from the Secretary.

(B) Such notice, in addition to meeting the requirements of paragraph (1), shall explain the basis for the Secretary's belief that the person to whom the notice is addressed is properly joined as a respondent.

(b) Investigative report and conciliation

(1) During the period beginning with the filing of such complaint and ending with the filing of a charge or a dismissal by the Secretary, the Secretary shall, to the extent feasible, engage in conciliation with respect to such complaint.

(2) A conciliation agreement arising out of such conciliation shall be an agreement between the respondent and the complainant, and shall be subject to approval by the Secretary.

(3) A conciliation agreement may provide for binding arbitration of the dispute arising from the complaint. Any such arbitration that results from a conciliation agreement may award appropriate relief, including monetary relief.

(4) Each conciliation agreement shall be made public unless the complainant and respondent otherwise agree and the Secretary determines that disclosure is not required to further the purposes of this subchapter.

(5)(A) At the end of each investigation under this section, the Secretary shall prepare a final investigative report containing—

(i) the names and dates of contacts with witnesses;

(ii) a summary and the dates of correspondence and other contacts with the aggrieved person and the respondent;

(iii) a summary description of other pertinent records;

(iv) a summary of witness statements; and

(v) answers to interrogatories.

(B) A final report under this paragraph may be amended if additional evidence is later discovered.

(c) Failure to comply with conciliation agreement Whenever the Secretary has reasonable cause to believe that a respondent has breached a conciliation agreement, the Secretary shall refer the matter to the Attorney General with a recommendation that a civil action be filed under section 3614 of this title for the enforcement of such agreement.

(d) Prohibitions and requirements with respect to disclosure of information

(1) Nothing said or done in the course of conciliation under this subchapter may be made public or used as evidence in a subsequent proceeding under this subchapter without the written consent of the persons concerned.

(2) Notwithstanding paragraph (1), the Secretary shall make available to the aggrieved person and the respondent, at any time, upon request following completion of the Secretary's investigation, information derived from an investigation and any final investigative report relating to that investigation.

(e) Prompt judicial action

(1) If the Secretary concludes at any time following the filing of a complaint that prompt judicial action is necessary to carry out the purposes of this subchapter, the Secretary may authorize a civil action for appropriate temporary or preliminary relief pending final disposition of the complaint under this section. Upon receipt of such an authorization, the Attorney General shall promptly commence and maintain such an action. Any temporary restraining order or other order granting preliminary or temporary relief shall be issued in accordance with the Federal Rules of Civil Procedure. The commencement of a civil action under this subsection does not affect the initiation or continuation of administrative proceedings under this section and section 3612 of this title.

(2) Whenever the Secretary has reason to believe that a basis may exist for the commencement of proceedings against any respondent under sections 3614(a) and 3614(c) of this title or for proceedings by any governmental licensing or supervisory authorities, the Secretary shall transmit the information upon which such belief is based to the Attorney General, or to such authorities, as the case may be.

(f) Referral for State or local proceedings

(1) Whenever a complaint alleges a discriminatory housing practice—

(A) within the jurisdiction of a State or local public agency; and

(B) as to which such agency has been certified by the Secretary under this subsection; the Secretary shall refer such complaint to that certified agency before taking any action with respect to such complaint.

(2) Except with the consent of such certified agency, the Secretary, after that referral is made, shall take no further action with respect to such complaint unless—

(A) the certified agency has failed to commence proceedings with respect to the complaint before the end of the 30th day after the date of such referral;

(B) the certified agency, having so commenced such proceedings, fails to carry forward such proceedings with reasonable promptness; or

(C) the Secretary determines that the certified agency no longer qualifies for certification under this subsection with respect to the relevant jurisdiction.

(3)(A) The Secretary may certify an agency under this subsection only if the Secretary determines that—

(i) the substantive rights protected by such agency in the jurisdiction with respect to which certification is to be made;

(ii) the procedures followed by such agency;

(iii) the remedies available to such agency; and

(iv) the availability of judicial review of such agency's action; are substantially equivalent to those created by and under this subchapter.

(B) Before making such certification, the Secretary shall take into account the current practices and past performance, if any, of such agency.

(4) During the period which begins on September 13, 1988, and ends 40 months after September 13, 1988, each agency certified (including an agency certified for interim referrals pursuant to 24 CFR 115.11, unless such agency is subsequently denied recognition under 24 CFR 115.7) for the purposes of this subchapter on the day before September 13, 1988, shall for the purposes of this subsection be considered certi-

fied under this subsection with respect to those matters for which such agency was certified on September 13, 1988. If the Secretary determines in an individual case that an agency has not been able to meet the certification requirements within this 40- month period due to exceptional circumstances, such as the infrequency of legislative sessions in that jurisdiction, the Secretary may extend such period by not more than 8 months.

(5) Not less frequently than every 5 years, the Secretary shall determine whether each agency certified under this subsection continues to qualify for certification. The Secretary shall take appropriate action with respect to any agency not so qualifying.

(g) Reasonable cause determination and effect

(1) The Secretary shall, within 100 days after the filing of the complaint (or, when the Secretary takes further action under subsection (f)(2) of this section with respect to a complaint, within 100 days after the commencement of such further action), determine based on the facts whether reasonable cause exists to believe that a discriminatory housing practice has occurred or is about to occur, unless it is impracticable to do so, or unless the Secretary has approved a conciliation agreement with respect to the complaint. If the Secretary is unable to make the determination within 100 days after the filing of the complaint (or, when the Secretary takes further action under subsection (f)(2) of this section with respect to a complaint, within 100 days after the commencement of such further action), the Secretary shall notify the complainant and respondent in writing of the reasons for not doing so.

(2)(A) If the Secretary determines that reasonable cause exists to believe that a discriminatory housing practice has occurred or is about to occur, the Secretary shall, except as provided in subparagraph (C), immediately issue a charge on behalf of the aggrieved person, for further proceedings under section 3612 of this title.

(B) Such charge—

(i) shall consist of a short and plain statement of the facts upon which the Secretary has found reasonable cause to believe that a discriminatory housing practice has occurred or is about to occur;

(ii) shall be based on the final investigative report; and (iii) need not be limited to the facts or grounds alleged in the complaint filed under subsection (a) of this section.

(C) If the Secretary determines that the matter involves the legality of any State or local zoning or other land use law or ordinance, the Secretary shall immediately refer the matter to the Attorney General for appropriate action under section 3614 of this title, instead of issuing such charge.

(3) If the Secretary determines that no reasonable cause exists to believe that a discriminatory housing practice has occurred or is about to occur, the Secretary shall promptly dismiss the complaint. The Secretary shall make public disclosure of each such dismissal.

(4) The Secretary may not issue a charge under this section regarding an alleged discriminatory housing practice after the beginning of the trial of a civil action commenced by the aggrieved party under an Act of Congress or a State law, seeking relief with respect to that discriminatory housing practice.

(h) Service of copies of charge

After the Secretary issues a charge under this section, the Secretary shall cause a copy thereof, together with information as to how to make an election under section 3612(a) of this title and the effect of such an election, to be served—

(1) on each respondent named in such charge, together with a notice of opportunity for a hearing at a time and place specified in the notice, unless that election is made; and

(2) on each aggrieved person on whose behalf the complaint was filed.

Sec. 3611. Subpoenas; giving of evidence

(a) In general

The Secretary may, in accordance with this subsection, issue subpoenas and order discovery in aid of investigations and hearings under this subchapter. Such subpoenas and discovery may be ordered to the same extent and subject to the same limitations as would apply if the subpoenas or discovery were ordered or served in aid of a civil action in the United States district court for the district in which the investigation is taking place.

(b) Witness fees

Witnesses summoned by a subpoena under this subchapter shall be entitled to the same witness and mileage fees as witnesses in proceedings in United States district courts. Fees payable to a witness summoned by a subpoena issued at the request of a party shall be paid by that party or, where a party is unable to pay the fees, by the Secretary.

(c) Criminal penalties

(1) Any person who willfully fails or neglects to attend and testify or to answer any lawful inquiry or to produce records, documents, or other evidence, if it is in such person's power to do so, in obedience to the subpoena or other lawful order under subsection (a) of this section, shall be fined not more than $100,000 or imprisoned not more than one year, or both.

(2) Any person who, with intent thereby to mislead another person in any proceeding under this subchapter—

(A) makes or causes to be made any false entry or statement of fact in any report, account, record, or other document produced pursuant to subpoena or other lawful order under subsection (a) of this section;

(B) willfully neglects or fails to make or to cause to be made full, true, and correct entries in such reports, accounts, records, or other documents; or

(C) willfully mutilates, alters, or by any other means falsifies any documentary evidence; shall be fined not more than $100,000 or imprisoned not more than one year, or both.

Sec. 3612. Enforcement by Secretary

(a) Election of judicial determination

When a charge is filed under section 3610 of this title, a complainant, a respondent, or an aggrieved person on whose behalf the complaint was filed, may elect to have the claims asserted in that charge decided in a civil action under subsection (o) of this section in lieu of a hearing under subsection (b) of this section. The election must be made not later than 20 days after the receipt by the electing person of service under section 3610(h) of this title or, in the case of the Secretary, not later than 20 days after such service. The person making such election shall give notice of doing so to the Secretary and to all other complainants and respondents to whom the charge relates.

(b) Administrative law judge hearing in absence of election

If an election is not made under subsection (a) of this section with respect to a charge filed under section 3610 of this title, the Secretary shall provide an opportunity for a hearing on the record with respect to a charge issued under section 3610 of this title. The Secretary shall delegate the conduct of a hearing under this section to an administrative law judge appointed under section 3105 of title 5. The administrative law judge shall conduct the hearing at a place in the vicinity in which the discriminatory housing practice is alleged to have occurred or to be about to occur.

(c) Rights of parties

At a hearing under this section, each party may appear in person, be represented by counsel, present evidence, cross-examine witnesses, and obtain the issuance of subpoenas under section 3611 of this title. Any aggrieved person may intervene as a party in the proceeding. The Federal Rules of Evidence apply to the presentation of evidence in such hearing as they would in a civil action in a United States district court.

(d) Expedited discovery and hearing

(1) Discovery in administrative proceedings under this section shall be conducted as expeditiously and inexpensively as possible, consistent with the need of all parties to obtain relevant evidence.

(2) A hearing under this section shall be conducted as expeditiously and inexpensively as possible, consistent with the needs and rights of the parties to obtain a fair hearing and a complete record.

(3) The Secretary shall, not later than 180 days after September 13, 1988, issue rules to implement this subsection.

(e) Resolution of charge

Any resolution of a charge before a final order under this section shall require the consent of the aggrieved person on whose behalf the charge is issued.

(f) Effect of trial of civil action on administrative proceedings

An administrative law judge may not continue administrative proceedings under this section regarding any alleged discriminatory housing practice after the beginning of the trial of a civil action commenced by the aggrieved party under an Act of Congress or a State law, seeking relief with respect to that discriminatory housing practice.

(g) Hearings, findings and conclusions, and order

(1) The administrative law judge shall commence the hearing under this section no later than 120 days following the issuance of the charge, unless it is impracticable to do so. If the administrative law judge is unable to commence the hearing within 120 days after the issuance of the charge, the administrative law judge shall notify the Secretary, the aggrieved person on whose behalf the charge was filed, and the respondent, in writing of the reasons for not doing so.

(2) The administrative law judge shall make findings of fact and conclusions of law within 60 days after the end of the hearing under this section, unless it is impracticable to do so. If the administrative law judge is unable to make findings of fact and conclusions of law within such period, or any succeeding 60-day period thereafter, the administrative law judge shall notify the Secretary, the aggrieved person on whose behalf the charge was filed, and the respondent, in writing of the reasons for not doing so.

(3) If the administrative law judge finds that a respondent has engaged or is about to engage in a discriminatory housing practice, such administrative law judge shall promptly issue an order for such relief as may be appropriate, which may include actual damages suffered by the aggrieved person and injunctive or other equitable relief. Such order may, to vindicate the public interest, assess a civil penalty against the respondent—

(A) in an amount not exceeding $10,000 if the respondent has not been adjudged to have committed any prior discriminatory housing practice;

(B) in an amount not exceeding $25,000 if the respondent has been adjudged to have committed one other discriminatory housing practice during the 5-year period ending on the date of the filing of this charge; and

(C) in an amount not exceeding $50,000 if the respondent has been adjudged to have committed 2 or more discriminatory housing practices during the 7-year period ending on the date of the filing of this charge; except that if the acts constituting the discriminatory housing practice that is the object of the charge are committed by the same natural person who has been previously adjudged to have committed acts constituting a discriminatory housing practice, then the civil penalties set forth in subparagraphs (B) and (C) may be imposed without regard to the period of time within which any subsequent discriminatory housing practice occurred.

(4) No such order shall affect any contract, sale, encumbrance, or lease consummated before the issuance of such order and involving a bona fide purchaser, encumbrancer, or tenant without actual notice of the charge filed under this subchapter.

(5) In the case of an order with respect to a discriminatory housing practice that occurred in the course of a business subject to a licensing or regulation by a governmental agency, the Secretary shall, not later than 30 days after the date of the issuance of such order (or, if such or-

der is judicially reviewed, 30 days after such order is in substance affirmed upon such review)—

(A) send copies of the findings of fact, conclusions of law, and the order, to that governmental agency; and

(B) recommend to that governmental agency appropriate disciplinary action (including, where appropriate, the suspension or revocation of the license of the respondent).

(6) In the case of an order against a respondent against whom another order was issued within the preceding 5 years under this section, the Secretary shall send a copy of each such order to the Attorney General.

(7) If the administrative law judge finds that the respondent has not engaged or is not about to engage in a discriminatory housing practice, as the case may be, such administrative law judge shall enter an order dismissing the charge. The Secretary shall make public disclosure of each such dismissal.

(h) Review by Secretary; service of final order

(1) The Secretary may review any finding, conclusion, or order issued under subsection (g) of this section. Such review shall be completed not later than 30 days after the finding, conclusion, or order is so issued; otherwise the finding, conclusion, or order becomes final.

(2) The Secretary shall cause the findings of fact and conclusions of law made with respect to any final order for relief under this section, together with a copy of such order, to be served on each aggrieved person and each respondent in the procceding.

(i) Judicial review

(1) Any party aggrieved by a final order for relief under this section granting or denying in whole or in part the relief sought.

(2) Notwithstanding such chapter, venue of the proceeding shall be in the judicial circuit in which the discriminatory housing practice is alleged to have occurred, and filing of the petition for review shall be not later than 30 days after the order is entered.

(j) Court enforcement of administrative order upon petition by Secretary

(1) The Secretary may petition any United States court of appeals for the circuit in which the discriminatory housing practice is alleged to have occurred or in which any respondent resides or transacts business for the enforcement of the order of the administrative law judge and for appropriate temporary relief or restraining order, by filing in such court

a written petition praying that such order be enforced and for appropriate temporary relief or restraining order.

(2) The Secretary shall file in court with the petition the record in the proceeding. A copy of such petition shall be forthwith transmitted by the clerk of the court to the parties to the proceeding before the administrative law judge.

(k) Relief which may be granted

(1) Upon the filing of a petition under subsection (i) or (j) of this section, the court may—

(A) grant to the petitioner, or any other party, such temporary relief, restraining order, or other order as the court deems just and proper;

(B) affirm, modify, or set aside, in whole or in part, the order, or remand the order for further proceedings; and

(C) enforce such order to the extent that such order is affirmed or modified.

(2) Any party to the proceeding before the administrative law judge may intervene in the court of appeals.

(3) No objection not made before the administrative law judge shall be considered by the court, unless the failure or neglect to urge such objection is excused because of extraordinary circumstances.

(l) Enforcement decree in absence of petition for review If no petition for review is filed under subsection (i) of this section before the expiration of 45 days after the date the administrative law judge's order is entered, the administrative law judge's findings of fact and order shall be conclusive in connection with any petition for enforcement—

(1) which is filed by the Secretary under subsection (j) of this section after the end of such day; or

(2) under subsection (m) of this section.

(m) Court enforcement of administrative order upon petition of any person entitled to relief

If before the expiration of 60 days after the date the administrative law judge's order is entered, no petition for review has been filed under subsection (i) of this section, and the Secretary has not sought enforcement of the order under subsection (j) of this section, any person entitled to relief under the order may petition for a decree enforcing the order in the United States court of appeals for the circuit in which the discriminatory housing practice is alleged to have occurred.

(n) Entry of decree

The clerk of the court of appeals in which a petition for enforcement is filed under subsection (l) or (m) of this section shall forthwith enter a decree enforcing the order and shall transmit a copy of such decree to the Secretary, the respondent named in the petition, and to any other parties to the proceeding before the administrative law judge.

(o) Civil action for enforcement when election is made for such civil action

(1) If an election is made under subsection (a) of this section, the Secretary shall authorize, and not later than 30 days after the election is made the Attorney General shall commence and maintain, a civil action on behalf of the aggrieved person in a United States district court seeking relief under this subsection. Venue for such civil action shall be determined under chapter 87 of title 28.

(2) Any aggrieved person with respect to the issues to be determined in a civil action under this subsection may intervene as of right in that civil action.

(3) In a civil action under this subsection, if the court finds that a discriminatory housing practice has occurred or is about to occur, the court may grant as relief any relief which a court could grant with respect to such discriminatory housing practice in a civil action under section 3613 of this title. Any relief so granted that would accrue to an aggrieved person in a civil action commenced by that aggrieved person under section 3613 of this title shall also accrue to that aggrieved person in a civil action under this subsection. If monetary relief is sought for the benefit of an aggrieved person who does not intervene in the civil action, the court shall not award such relief if that aggrieved person has not complied with discovery orders entered by the court.

(p) Attorney's fees

In any administrative proceeding brought under this section, or any court proceeding arising therefrom, or any civil action under this section, the administrative law judge or the court, as the case may be, in its discretion, may allow the prevailing party, other than the United States, a reasonable attorney's fee and costs. The United States shall be liable for such fees and costs to the extent provided by section 504 of title 5 or by section 2412 of title 28.

Sec. 3613. Enforcement by private persons

(a) Civil action

(1)(A) An aggrieved person may commence a civil action in an appropriate United States district court or State court not later than 2 years after the occurrence or the termination of an alleged discriminatory housing practice, or the breach of a conciliation agreement entered into under this subchapter, whichever occurs last, to obtain appropriate relief with respect to such discriminatory housing practice or breach.

(B) The computation of such 2-year period shall not include any time during which an administrative proceeding under this subchapter was pending with respect to a complaint or charge under this subchapter based upon such discriminatory housing practice. This subparagraph does not apply to actions arising from a breach of a conciliation agreement.

(2) An aggrieved person may commence a civil action under this subsection whether or not a complaint has been filed under section 3610(a) of this title and without regard to the status of any such complaint, but if the Secretary or a State or local agency has obtained a conciliation agreement with the consent of an aggrieved person, no action may be filed under this subsection by such aggrieved person with respect to the alleged discriminatory housing practice which forms the basis for such complaint except for the purpose of enforcing the terms of such an agreement.

(3) An aggrieved person may not commence a civil action under this subsection with respect to an alleged discriminatory housing practice which forms the basis of a charge issued by the Secretary if an administrative law judge has commenced a hearing on the record under this subchapter with respect to such charge.

(b) Appointment of attorney by court Upon application by a person alleging a discriminatory housing practice or a person against whom such a practice is alleged, the court may—

(1) appoint an attorney for such person; or

(2) authorize the commencement or continuation of a civil action under subsection (a) of this section without the payment of fees, costs, or security, if in the opinion of the court such person is financially unable to bear the costs of such action.

(c) Relief which may be granted

(1) In a civil action under subsection (a) of this section, if the court finds that a discriminatory housing practice has occurred or is about to

occur, the court may award to the plaintiff actual and punitive damages, and subject to subsection (d) of this section, may grant as relief, as the court deems appropriate, any permanent or temporary injunction, temporary restraining order, or other order (including an order enjoining the defendant from engaging in such practice or ordering such affirmative action as may be appropriate).

(2) In a civil action under subsection (a) of this section, the court, in its discretion, may allow the prevailing party, other than the United States, a reasonable attorney's fee and costs. The United States shall be liable for such fees and costs to the same extent as a private person.

(d) Effect on certain sales, encumbrances, and rentals

Relief granted under this section shall not affect any contract, sale, encumbrance, or lease consummated before the granting of such relief and involving a bona fide purchaser, encumbrancer, or tenant, without actual notice of the filing of a complaint with the Secretary or civil action under this subchapter.

(e) Intervention by Attorney General

Upon timely application, the Attorney General may intervene in such civil action, if the Attorney General certifies that the case is of general public importance. Upon such intervention the Attorney General may obtain such relief as would be available to the Attorney General under section 3614(e) of this title in a civil action to which such section applies.

Sec. 3614. Enforcement by Attorney General

(a) Pattern or practice cases

Whenever the Attorney General has reasonable cause to believe that any person or group of persons is engaged in a pattern or practice of resistance to the full enjoyment of any of the rights granted by this subchapter, or that any group of persons has been denied any of the rights granted by this subchapter and such denial raises an issue of general public importance, the Attorney General may commence a civil action in any appropriate United States district court.

(b) On referral of discriminatory housing practice or conciliation agreement for enforcement

(1)(A) The Attorney General may commence a civil action in any appropriate United States district court for appropriate relief with respect to a discriminatory housing practice referred to the Attorney General by the Secretary under section 3610(g) of this title.

(B) A civil action under this paragraph may be commenced not later than the expiration of 18 months after the date of the occurrence or the termination of the alleged discriminatory housing practice.

(2)(A) The Attorney General may commence a civil action in any appropriate United States district court for appropriate relief with respect to breach of a conciliation agreement referred to the Attorney General by the Secretary under section 3610(c) of this title.

(B) A civil action may be commenced under this paragraph not later than the expiration of 90 days after the referral of the alleged breach under section 3610(c) of this title.

(c) Enforcement of subpoenas

The Attorney General, on behalf of the Secretary, or other party at whose request a subpoena is issued, under this subchapter, may enforce such subpoena in appropriate proceedings in the United States district court for the district in which the person to whom the subpoena was addressed resides, was served, or transacts business.

(d) Relief which may be granted in civil actions under subsections (a) and (b)

(1) In a civil action under subsection (a) or (b) of this section, the court—

(A) may award such preventive relief, including a permanent or temporary injunction, restraining order, or other order against the person responsible for a violation of this subchapter as is necessary to assure the full enjoyment of the rights granted by this subchapter;

(B) may award such other relief as the court deems appropriate, including monetary damages to persons aggrieved; and

(C) may, to vindicate the public interest, assess a civil penalty against the respondent—

(i) in an amount not exceeding $50,000, for a first violation; and

(ii) in an amount not exceeding $100,000, for any subsequent violation.

(2) In a civil action under this section, the court, in its discretion, may allow the prevailing party, other than the United States, a reasonable attorney's fee and costs. The United States shall be liable for such fees and costs to the extent provided by section 2412 of title 28.

(e) Intervention in civil actions

Upon timely application, any person may intervene in a civil action commenced by the Attorney General under subsection (a) or (b) of this section which involves an alleged discriminatory housing practice with respect to which such person is an aggrieved person or a conciliation agreement to which such person is a party. The court may grant such appropriate relief to any such intervening party as is authorized to be granted to a plaintiff in a civil action under section 3613 of this title.

Sec. 3615. Effect on State laws

Nothing in this subchapter shall be construed to invalidate or limit any law of a State or political subdivision of a State, or of any other jurisdiction in which this subchapter shall be effective, that grants, guarantees, or protects the same rights as are granted by this subchapter; but any law of a State, a political subdivision, or other such jurisdiction that purports to require or permit any action that would be a discriminatory housing practice under this subchapter shall to that extent be invalid.

Sec. 3616. Cooperation with State and local agencies administering fair housing laws; utilization of services and personnel; reimbursement; written agreements; publication in Federal Register

The Secretary may cooperate with State and local agencies charged with the administration of State and local fair housing laws and, with the consent of such agencies, utilize the services of such agencies and their employees and, notwithstanding any other provision of law, may reimburse such agencies and their employees for services rendered to assist him in carrying out this subchapter. In furtherance of such cooperative efforts, the Secretary may enter into written agreements with such State or local agencies. All agreements and terminations thereof shall be published in the Federal Register.

Sec. 3616a. Fair housing initiatives program

(a) In general

The Secretary of Housing and Urban Development (in this section referred to as the "Secretary") may make grants to, or (to the extent of amounts provided in appropriation Acts) enter into contracts or cooperative agreements with, State or local governments or their agencies, public or private nonprofit organizations or institutions, or other public or private entities that are formulating or carrying out programs to prevent or eliminate discriminatory housing practices, to develop, implement, carry out, or coordinate—

(1) programs or activities designed to obtain enforcement of the rights granted by title VIII of the Act of April 11, 1968 (42 U.S.C.

3601 et seq.) (commonly referred to as the Civil Rights Act of 1968), or by State or local laws that provide rights and remedies for alleged discriminatory housing practices that are substantially equivalent to the rights and remedies provided in such title VIII, through such appropriate judicial or administrative proceedings (including informal methods of conference, conciliation, and persuasion) as are available therefor; and

(2) education and outreach programs designed to inform the public concerning rights and obligations under the laws referred to in paragraph (1).

(b) Private enforcement initiatives

(1) In general

The Secretary shall use funds made available under this subsection to conduct, through contracts with private nonprofit fair housing enforcement organizations, investigations of violations of the rights granted under title VIII of the Civil Rights Act of 1968 (42 U.S.C. 3601 et seq.), and such enforcement activities as appropriate to remedy such violations. The Secretary may enter into multiyear contracts and take such other action as is appropriate to enhance the effectiveness of such investigations and enforcement activities.

(2) Activities

The Secretary shall use funds made available under this subsection to conduct, through contracts with private nonprofit fair housing enforcement organizations, a range of investigative and enforcement activities designed to—

(A) carry out testing and other investigative activities in accordance with subsection (b)(1) of this section, including building the capacity for housing investigative activities in unserved or underserved areas;

(B) discover and remedy discrimination in the public and private real estate markets and real estate-related transactions, including, but not limited to, the making or purchasing of loans or the provision of other financial assistance sales and rentals of housing and housing advertising;

(C) carry out special projects, including the development of prototypes to respond to new or sophisticated forms of discrimination against persons protected under title VIII of the Civil Rights Act of 1968 (42 U.S.C. 3601 et seq.);

(D) provide technical assistance to local fair housing organizations, and assist in the formation and development of new fair housing organizations; and

(E) provide funds for the costs and expenses of litigation, including expert witness fees.

(c) Funding of fair housing organizations

(1) In general

The Secretary shall use funds made available under this section to enter into contracts or cooperative agreements with qualified fair housing enforcement organizations, other private nonprofit fair housing enforcement organizations, and nonprofit groups organizing to build their capacity to provide fair housing enforcement, for the purpose of supporting the continued development or implementation of initiatives which enforce the rights granted under title VIII of the Civil Rights Act of 1968 (42 U.S.C. 3601 et seq.), as amended. Contracts or cooperative agreements may not provide more than 50 percent of the operating budget of the recipient organization for any one year.

(2) Capacity enhancement

The Secretary shall use funds made available under this section to help establish, organize, and build the capacity of fair housing enforcement organizations, particularly in those areas of the country which are currently underserved by fair housing enforcement organizations as well as those areas where large concentrations of protected classes exist. For purposes of meeting the objectives of this paragraph, the Secretary may enter into contracts or cooperative agreements with qualified fair housing enforcement organizations. The Secretary shall establish annual goals which reflect the national need for private fair housing enforcement organizations.

(d) Education and outreach

(1) In general

The Secretary, through contracts with one or more qualified fair housing enforcement organizations, other fair housing enforcement organizations, and other nonprofit organizations representing groups of persons protected under title VIII of the Civil Rights Act of 1968 (42 U.S.C. 3601 et seq.), shall establish a national education and outreach program. The national program shall be designed to provide a centralized, coordinated effort for the development and dissemination of fair housing media products, including—

(A) public service announcements, both audio and video;

(B) television, radio and print advertisements;

(C) posters; and

(D) pamphlets and brochures.

The Secretary shall designate a portion of the amounts provided in subsection (g)(4) of this section for a national program specifically for activities related to the annual national fair housing month. The Secretary shall encourage cooperation with real estate industry organizations in the national education and outreach program. The Secretary shall also encourage the dissemination of educational information and technical assistance to support compliance with the housing adaptability and accessibility guidelines contained in the Fair Housing Act Amendments of 1988.

(2) Regional and local programs

The Secretary, through contracts with fair housing enforcement organizations, other nonprofit organizations representing groups of persons protected under title VIII of the Civil Rights Act of 1968 (42 U.S.C. 3601 et seq.), State and local agencies certified by the Secretary under section 810(f) of the Fair Housing Act (42 U.S.C. 3610(f)), or other public or private entities that are formulating or carrying out programs to prevent or eliminate discriminatory housing practices, shall establish or support education and outreach programs at the regional and local levels.

(3) Community-based programs

The Secretary shall provide funding to fair housing organizations and other nonprofit organizations representing groups of persons protected under title VIII of the Civil Rights Act of 1968, or other public or private entities that are formulating or carrying out programs to prevent or eliminate discriminatory housing practices, to support community-based education and outreach activities, including school, church, and community presentations, conferences, and other educational activities.

Sec. 3617. Interference, coercion, or intimidation

It shall be unlawful to coerce, intimidate, threaten, or interfere with any person in the exercise or enjoyment of, or on account of his having exercised or enjoyed, or on account of his having aided or encouraged any other person in the exercise or enjoyment of, any right granted or protected by section 3603, 3604, 3605, or 3606 of this title.

Sec. 3631. Violations; penalties

Whoever, whether or not acting under color of law, by force or threat of force willfully injuries, intimidates or interferes with, or attempts to injure, intimidate or interfere with—

(a) any person because of his race, color, religion, sex, handicap (as such term is defined in section 3602 of this title), familial status (as such term is defined in section 3602 of this title), or national origin and because he is or has been selling, purchasing, renting, financing, occupying, or contracting or negotiating for the sale, purchase, rental, financing or occupation of any dwelling, or applying for or participating in any service, organization, or facility relating to the business of selling or renting dwellings; or

(b) any person because he is or has been, or in order to intimidate such person or any other person or any class of persons from—

(1) participating, without discrimination on account of race, color, religion, sex, handicap (as such term is defined in section 3602 of this title), familial status (as such term is defined in section 3602 of this title), or national origin, in any of the activities, services, organizations or facilities described in subsection (a) of this section; or

(2) affording another person or class of persons opportunity or protection so to participate; or

(c) any citizen because he is or has been, or in order to discourage such citizen or any other citizen from lawfully aiding or encouraging other persons to participate, without discrimination on account of race, color, religion, sex, handicap (as such term is defined in section 3602 of this title), familial status (as such term is defined in section 3602 of this title), or national origin, in any of the activities, services, organizations or facilities described in subsection (a) of this section, or participating lawfully in speech or peaceful assembly opposing any denial of the opportunity to so participate—shall be fined under title 18 or imprisoned not more than one year, or both; and if bodily injury results from the acts committed in violation of this section or if such acts include the use, attempted use, or threatened use of a dangerous weapon, explosives, or fire shall be fined under title 18 or imprisoned not more than ten years, or both; and if death results from the acts committed in violation of this section or if such acts include kidnapping or an attempt to kidnap, aggravated sexual abuse or an attempt to commit aggravated sexual abuse, or an attempt to kill, shall be fined under title 18 or imprisoned for any term of years or for life, or both.

APPENDIX 12:
DIRECTORY OF HUD FAIR HOUSING ENFORCEMENT CENTERS

REGION	ADDRESS	TELEPHONE	TTY
CONNECTICUT, MAIN, MASSACHUSETTS, NEW HAMPSHIRE, RHODE ISLAND, VERMONT	Fair Housing Enforcement Center U.S. Department of Housing and Urban Development (HUD) 10 Causeway Street, Room 321 Boston, MA 02222-1092	617-565-5308/ 800-827-5005	617-565-5453
NEW JERSEY, NEW YORK	Fair Housing Enforcement Center U.S. Department of Housing and Urban Development (HUD) 26 Federal Plaza, Room 3532 New York, NY 10278-0068	212-264-9610/ 800-496-4294	212-264-0927

REGION	ADDRESS	TELEPHONE	TTY
DELAWARE, DISTRICT OF COLUMBIA, MARYLAND, PENNSYLVANIA, VIRGINIA, WEST VIRGINIA	Fair Housing Enforcement Center U.S. Department of Housing and Urban Development (HUD) The Wanamaker Building 100 Penn Square East Philadelphia, PA 19107-3380	215-656-0660/ 888-799-2085,	215-656-3450
ALABAMA, CARIBBEAN, FLORIDA, GEORGIA, KENTUCKY, MISSISSIPPI, NORTH CAROLINA, SOUTH CAROLINA, TENNESSEE	Fair Housing Enforcement Center U.S. Department of Housing and Urban Development (HUD) Richard B. Russell Federal Building 75 Spring Street SW, Room 230 Atlanta, GA 30303-3388	404-331-5140/ 800-440-8091	404-730-2654
ILLINOIS, INDIANA, MICHIGAN, MINNESOTA, OHIO, WISCONSIN	Fair Housing Enforcement Center U.S. Department of Housing and Urban Development (HUD) Ralph H. Metcalfe Federal Building 77 West Jackson Boulevard, Room 2101 Chicago, IL 60604-3507	312-353-7776/ 800-765-9372	312-353-7143
ARKANSAS, LOUISIANA, NEW MEXICO, OKLAHOMA, TEXAS	Fair Housing Enforcement Center U.S. Department of Housing and Urban Development (HUD) 1600 Throckmorton, Room 502 Forth Worth, TX 76113-2905	817-978-9270/ 800-498-9371	817-978-9274
IOWA, KANSAS, MISSOURI, NEBRASKA	Fair Housing Enforcement Center U.S. Department of Housing and Urban Development (HUD) Gateway Tower II 400 State Avenue, Room 200 Kansas City, KS 66101-2406	913-551-6958/ 800-743-5323	913-551-6972

REGION	ADDRESS	TELEPHONE	TTY
COLORADO, MONTANA, NORTH DAKOTA, SOUTH DAKOTA, UTAH, WYOMING	Fair Housing Enforcement Center U.S. Department of Housing and Urban Development (HUD) 633 17th Street Denver, CO 80202-3607	303-672-5437/ 800-877-7353	303-672-5248
ARIZONA, CALIFORNIA, HAWAII, NEVADA	Fair Housing Enforcement Center U.S. Department of Housing and Urban Development (HUD) Phillip Burton Federal Building and U.S. Courthouse 450 Golden Gate Avenue San Francisco, CA 94102-3448	415-436-8400/ 800-347-3739	415-436-6594
ALASKA, IDAHO, OREGON, WASHINGTON	Fair Housing Enforcement Center U.S. Department of Housing and Urban Development (HUD) Seattle Federal Office Building 909 First Avenue Room 205 Seattle, WA 98104-1000	206-220-5170/ 800-877-0246	206-220-5185

Source: United States Department of Housing and Urban Development

APPENDIX 13:
SAMPLE HUD HOUSING DISCRIMINATION COMPLAINT FORM

If you don't report discrimination, it can't be stopped!

Housing Discrimination Information Form

- If you believe your rights have been violated, HUD or a State or local fair housing agency is ready to help you file a complaint.

- You have one year from the date of the alleged act of discrimination to file your complaint.

- After your information is received, we will contact you to discuss the concerns you raise.

Instructions: (Please type or print.) Read this form carefully. Try to answer all questions. If you do not know the answer or a question does not apply to you, leave the space blank. You have one year from the date of the alleged discrimination to file a complaint. Your form should be signed and dated. Use reverse side of this page if you need more space to respond.

Keep this information for your records.

Date you mailed your information to HUD:

Address to which you sent the information:
  Street:

City: State: Zip Code:

If you have not heard from HUD or a fair housing agency within three weeks from the date you mail this form, you may call to inquire about the status of your complaint. See addresses and telephone listings on the last page.

Your Name:	Best time to call:	Your Daytime Phone No:
Your Address:		Evening Phone No:
City:	State:	Zip Code:

Who else can we call if we cannot reach you?

1 Contact's Name:	Daytime Phone No:
Best time to call:	Evening Phone No:
2 Contact's Name:	Daytime Phone No:
Best time to call:	Evening Phone No:

1. **What** happened to you? How were you discriminated against? For example: were you refused an opportunity to rent or buy housing? Denied a loan? Told that housing was not available when in fact it was? Treated differently from others seeking housing? State briefly what happened.

2. **Why** do you believe you are being discriminated against?

It is a violation of the law to deny you your housing rights for any of the following factors: • race • color • religion • sex • national origin • familial status (families with children under 18) • disability.

For example: were you denied housing **because of** your race? Were you denied a mortgage loan **because of** your religion? Or turned down for an apartment **because** you have children? Were you harassed because you assisted someone in obtaining their fair housing rights? Briefly explain why you think your housing rights were denied **because of** any the factors listed above.

3. **Who** do you believe discriminated against you? Was it a landlord, owner, bank, real estate agent, broker, company, or organization?

Name:

Address:

4. **Where** did the alleged act of discrimination occur? Provide the address. For example: Was it at a rental unit? Single family home? Public or Assisted Housing? A Mobile Home? Did it occur at a bank or other lending institution?

Address:

City: State: Zip Code:

5. **When** did the last act of discrimination occur? Enter the date _____/_____/_____
Is the alleged discrimination continuous or on going?

☐ Yes   ☐ No

Signature: Date:

X _____

Send this form to HUD or to the fair housing agency where the alleged act of discrimination occurred.
If you are unable to complete this form, you may call the office nearest you.
See addresses and telephone numbers listed on the back page.

The information collected here will be used to investigate and to process housing discrimination complaints. The information may be disclosed to the United States Department of Justice for its use in the filing of pattern and practice suits of housing discrimination or the prosecution of the person(s) who committed the discrimination where violence is involved; and to State or local fair housing agencies that administer substantially equivalent fair housing laws for complaint processing.

Public Reporting Burden for this collection of information is estimated to average 20 minutes per response, including the time for reviewing instructions, searching existing data sources, gathering and maintaining the data needed, and completing and reviewing the collection of information.

Disclosure of this information is voluntary. Failure to provide some or all of the requested information will result in delay or denial of HUD assistance.

This agency may not collect this information, and you are not required to complete this form, unless it displays a currently valid OMB control number.

Privacy Act Statement The Department of Housing and Urban Development is authorized to collect this information by Title VIII of the Civil Rights Act of 1968, as amended by the Fair Housing Amendments Act of 1988, (P.L. 100-430); Title VI of the Civil Rights Act of 1964, (P.L. 88-352); Section 504 of the Rehabilitation Act of 1973, as amended, (P.L. 93-112); Section 109 of Title I - Housing and Community Development Act of 1974, as amended, (P.L. 97-35); Americans with Disabilities Act of 1990, (P.L. 101-336); and by the Age Discrimination Act of 1975, as amended, (42 U.S.C. 6103).

For **Connecticut, Maine, Massachusetts, New Hampshire, Rhode Island, and Vermont:**
Fair Housing Enforcement Center
U.S. Department HUD
10 Causeway Street, Room 321
Boston, MA 02222-1092
(617) 565-5308
1-800-827-5005
TTY (617) 565-5453

For **New Jersey and New York:**
Fair Housing Enforcement Center
U.S. Department HUD
26 Federal Plaza, Room 3532
New York, NY 10278-0068
(212) 264-9610
1-800-496-4294
TTY (212) 264-0927

For **Delaware, District of Columbia, Maryland, Pennsylvania, Virginia, and West Virginia:**
Fair Housing Enforcement Center
U.S. Department HUD
The Wanamaker Building
100 Penn Square East
Philadelphia, PA 19107-3380
(215) 656-0660
1-888-799-2085
TTY (215) 656-3450

For **Alabama, the Caribbean, Florida, Georgia, Kentucky, Mississippi, North Carolina, South Carolina, and Tennessee:**
Fair Housing Enforcement Center
U.S. Department HUD
Richard B. Russell Federal Bldg.
75 Spring Street, SW, Room 230
Atlanta, GA 30303-3388
(404) 331-5140
1-800-440-8091
TTY (404) 730-2654

For **Illinois, Indiana, Michigan, Minnesota, Ohio, and Wisconsin:**
Fair Housing Enforcement Center
U.S. Department HUD
Ralph H. Metcalfe Federal Bldg.
77 West Jackson Boulevard,
Room 2101
Chicago, IL 60604-3507
(312) 353-7776
1-800-765-9372
TTY (312) 353-7143

For **Arkansas, Louisiana, New Mexico, Oklahoma, and Texas:**
Fair Housing Enforcement Center
U.S. Department HUD
1600 Throckmorton, Room 502
Forth Worth, TX 76113-2905
(817) 978-9270
1-800-498-9371
TTY (817) 978-9274

For **Iowa, Kansas, Missouri and Nebraska:**
Fair Housing Enforcement Center
U.S. Department HUD
Gateway Tower II
400 State Avenue, Room 200
Kansas City, KA 66101-2406
(913) 551-6958
1-800-743-5323
TTY (913) 551-6972

For **Colorado, Montana, North Dakota, South Dakota, Utah, and Wyoming:**
Fair Housing Enforcement Center
U.S. Department HUD
633 17th Street
Denver, CO 80202-3607
(303) 672-5437
1-800-877-7353
TTY (303) 672-5248

For **Arizona, California, Hawaii, and Nevada:**
Fair Housing Enforcement Center
U.S. Department HUD
Phillip Burton Federal Building
and U.S. Courthouse
450 Golden Gate Avenue
San Francisco, CA 94102-3448
(415) 436-8400
1-800-347-3739
TTY (415) 436-6594

For **Alaska, Idaho, Oregon, and Washington:**
Fair Housing Enforcement Center
U.S. Department HUD
Seattle Federal Office Building
909 First Avenue, Room 205
Seattle, WA 98104-1000
(206) 220-5170
1-800-877-0246
TTY (206) 220-5185

GLOSSARY

Acceleration Clause A common provision of a mortgage or note providing the holder with the right to demand that the entire outstanding balance is immediately due and usually payable in the event of default.

Acceptance of Deed The physical taking of the deed by the grantee.

Acceptance of Offer The seller's agreement to the terms of the agreement of sale.

Accrued Interest Interest earned but not yet paid.

Acknowledgment A formal declaration of one's signature before a notary public.

Adjustable Rate Mortgage Loans (ARM) Loans with interest rates that are adjusted periodically based on changes in a pre-selected index.

Adjustment Interval On an ARM loan, the time between changes in the interest rate or monthly payment.

Agreement of Sale Contract signed by buyer and seller stating the terms and conditions under which a property will be sold.

Alternative Documentation	A method of documenting a loan file that relies on information the borrower is likely to be able to provide instead of waiting on verification sent to third parties for confirmation of statements made in the application.
Amortization	Repayment of a loan with periodic payments of both principal and interest calculated to payoff the loan at the end of a fixed period of time.
Amortized Mortgage	A mortgage in which repayment is made according to a plan requiring the payment of certain amounts at specified times so that all the debt is repaid at the end of the term.
Annual Percentage Rate (APR)	The cost of credit expressed as a yearly rate. The annual percentage rate is often not the same as the interest rate. It is a percentage that results from an equation considering the amount financed, the finance charges, and the term of the loan.
Appraisal	A written estimate of a property's current market value completed by an impartial party with knowledge of real estate markets.
Appraisal Fee	A fee charged by a licensed, certified appraiser to render an opinion of market value as of a specific date.
Assignment	The transfer of ownership, rights, or interests in property by one person, the assignor, to another, the assignee.
Assumption	A method of selling real estate where the buyer of the property agrees to become responsible for the repayment of an existing loan on the property.
Balloon Mortgage	Balloon mortgage loans are short-term fixed-rate loans with fixed monthly payments for a set number of years followed by one large final "balloon" payment for all of the remainder of the principal.

Bankruptcy	A proceeding in a federal court to relieve certain debts of a person or a business unable to pay its debts.
Bargain and Sale Deed with Covenant	A deed conveying real property with a covenant which warrants title against grantor's acts.
Bargain and Sale Deed without Covenant	A deed conveying real property without any covenants warranting title.
Blanket Mortgage	A mortgage that covers more than one parcel of real estate.
Borrower	Also known as the mortgagor, refers to the individual who applies for and receives funds in the form of a loan and is obligated to repay the loan in full under the terms of the loan.
Broker	An individual who brings buyers and sellers together and assists in negotiating contracts for a client.
Buy-Down Mortgage	A mortgage loan with a below-market rate for a period of time.
Buyer's Market	Market conditions that favor buyers.
Call Option	A provision of a note which allows the lender to require repayment of the loan in full before the end of the loan term. The option may be exercised due to breach of the terms of the loan or at the discretion of the lender.
Cash Out	Any cash received when you get a new loan that is larger than the remaining balance of your current mortgage, based upon the equity you have already built up in the house. The cash out amount is calculated by subtracting the sum of the old loan and fees from the new mortgage loan.

Cashier's Check Also known as a bank check, refers to a check whose payment is guaranteed because it was paid for in advance and is drawn on the bank's account instead of the customer's.

Ceiling The maximum allowable interest rate of an adjustable rate mortgage.

Certificate of Eligibility Document issued by the Veterans Administration to qualified veterans which verifies a veteran's eligibility for a VA guaranteed loan.

Certificate of Title Written opinion of the status of title to a property, given by an attorney or title company. This certificate does not offer the protection given by title insurance.

Certificate of Veteran Status FHA form filled out by the VA to establish a borrower's eligibility for an FHA Vet loan.

Chain of Title The chronological order of conveyance of a property from the original owner to the present owner.

Closing Also known as settlement, refers to the conclusion of a real estate transaction and includes the delivery of the security instrument, signing of legal documents and the disbursement of the funds necessary to the sale of the home or loan transaction.

Closing Costs Also known as settlement costs, refers to the costs for services that must be performed before the loan can be initiated, such as title fees, recording fees, appraisal fee, credit report fee, pest inspection, attorney's fees, and surveying fees.

Collateral Assets pledged as security for a debt, such as a home.

Commission Money paid to a real estate agent or broker for negotiating a real estate or loan transaction.

Commitment	A promise to lend and a statement by the lender of the terms and conditions under which a loan is made.
Condominium	A form of property ownership in which the home-owner holds title to an individual dwelling unit and a proportionate interest in common areas and facilities of a multi-unit project.
Conforming Loan	A mortgage loan which meets all requirements to be eligible for purchase by federal agencies such as FNMA and FHLMC.
Consideration	Something of value exchanged between parties to a contract—a requirement for a valid contract.
Contingency	A condition which must be satisfied before a contract is legally binding.
Contract of Sale	The agreement between the buyer and seller on the purchase price, terms, and conditions of a sale.
Conventional Loan	A mortgage made by a financial institution which loan is not insured or guaranteed by the government.
Conversion Clause	A provision in some ARMs that allows you to change an ARM to a fixed-rate loan, usually after the first adjustment period. The new fixed rate will be set at current rates, and there may be a charge for the conversion feature.
Convertible ARMs	A type of ARM loan with the option to convert to a fixed-rate loan during a given time period.
Conveyance	The document used to effect a transfer, such as a deed, or mortgage.
Cooperative	Ownership of stock in a corporation which owns property that is subdivided into individual units.

Cost of Funds Index (COFI) An index of the weighted-average interest rate paid by savings institutions for sources of funds, usually by members of the 11th Federal Home Loan Bank District.

Covenant An undertaking by one or more parties to a deed.

Credit Report A report detailing the credit history of a prospective borrower that's used to help determine borrower creditworthiness.

Deed Legal document by which title to real property is transferred from one owner to another. The deed contains a description of the property, and is signed, witnessed, and delivered to the buyer at closing.

Deed of Trust A legal document that conveys title to real property to a third party. The third party holds title until the owner of the property has repaid the debt in full.

Default Failure to meet legal obligations in a contract, including failure to make payments on a loan.

Delinquency Failure to make payments as agreed in the loan agreement.

Discount Points Points are an up-front fee paid to the lender at the time that you get your loan. Each point equals one percent of your total loan amount. Points and interest rates are inherently connected: in general, the more points you pay, the lower the interest rate you get. However, the more points one pays, the more cash they need up front since points are paid in cash at closing.

Down Payment The amount of a home's purchase price one needs to supply up front in cash to get a loan.

Due-on-Sale Clause Provision in a mortgage or deed of trust allowing the lender to demand immediate payment of the loan balance upon sale of the property.

Earnest Money	Deposit made by a buyer towards the down payment in evidence of good faith when the purchase agreement is signed.
Equal Credit Opportunity Act (ECOA)	Federal law requiring creditors to make credit equally available without discrimination based on race, color, religion, national origin, age, sex, marital status or receipt of income from public assistance programs.
Equity	The difference between the current market value of a property and the total debt obligations against the property. On a new mortgage loan, the down payment represents the equity in the property.
Escrow	A transaction in which a third party acts as the agent for seller and buyer, or for borrower and lender, in handling legal documents and disbursement of funds.
Escrow Account	An account held by the lender to which the borrower pays monthly installments, collected as part of the monthly mortgage payment, for annual expenses such as taxes and insurance. The lender disburses escrow account funds on behalf of the borrower when they become due. Also known as Impound Account.
Escrow Agent	A person with fiduciary responsibility to the buyer and seller, or the borrower and lender, to ensure that the terms of the purchase/sale or loan are carried out.
Executor's Deed	A deed given by an executor or other fiduciary which conveys real property.
Fannie Mae	A common nickname for the Federal National Mortgage Association.
Federal Deposit Insurance Corporation (FDIC)	Independent deposit insurance agency created by Congress to maintain stability and public confidence in the nation's banking system.

Federal Home Loan Mortgage Corporation (FHLMC)
Also known as "Freddie Mac," refers to the federal agency which buys loans that are underwritten to its specific guidelines, an industry standard for residential conventional lending.

Federal Housing Administration (FHA)
A federal agency within the Department of Housing and Urban Development (HUD), which insures residential mortgage loans made by private lenders and sets standards for underwriting mortgage loans.

Federal National Mortgage Association (FNMA)
Also known as "Fannie Mae," refers to the federal agency which buys loans that are underwritten to its specific guidelines, an industry standard for residential conventional lending.

Fee Simple
Absolute ownership of real property.

FHA Loans
Fixed or adjustable rate loans insured by the U.S. Department of Housing and Urban Development.

First Mortgage
A mortgage which is in first lien position, taking priority over all other liens. In the case of a foreclosure, the first mortgage will be repaid before any other mortgages.

Fixed Rate
An interest rate which is fixed for the term of the loan.

Fixed-Rate Loans
Fixed-rate loans have interest rates that do not change over the life of the loan. As a result, monthly payments for principal and interest are also fixed for the life of the loan.

Flood Insurance
Insurance that compensates for physical damage to a property by flood. Typically not covered under standard hazard insurance.

Forbearance
The act by the lender of refraining from taking legal action on a mortgage loan that is delinquent.

Foreclosure
Legal process by which a mortgaged property may be sold to pay off a mortgage loan that is in default.

Full Covenant and Warranty Deed
A deed conveying real property which contains a covenant that warrants title by each previous holder of warranty deeds.

Good Faith Estimate
Written estimate of the settlement costs the borrower will likely have to pay at closing. Under the Real Estate Settlement Procedures Act (RESPA), the lender is required to provide this disclosure to the borrower within three days of receiving a loan application.

Grace Period
Period of time during which a loan payment may be made after its due date without incurring a late penalty. The grace period is specified as part of the terms of the loan in the Note.

Grantee
One who receives a conveyance of real property by deed.

Grantor
One who conveys real property by deed.

Gross Income
Total income before taxes or expenses are deducted.

Hazard Insurance
Protects the insured against loss due to fire or other natural disaster in exchange for a premium paid to the insurer.

Housing and Urban Development (HUD)
A federal government agency established to implement federal housing and community development programs; oversees the Federal Housing Administration.

HUD-1 Uniform Settlement Statement
A standard form which itemizes the closing costs associated with purchasing a home or refinancing a loan.

Impound Account
Also known as an escrow account, refers to an account held by the lender to which the borrower pays monthly installments, collected as part of the monthly mortgage payment, for annual expenses such as taxes and insurance. The lender disburses impound account funds on behalf of the borrower when they become due.

Index	A published rate used by lenders that serves as the basis for determining interest rate changes on ARM loans.
Initial Rate	The rate charged during the first interval of an ARM loan.
Interest	Charge paid for borrowing money, calculated as a percentage of the remaining balance of the amount borrowed.
Interest Rate	The annual rate of interest on the loan, expressed as a percentage of 100.
Interest Rate Cap	Consumer safeguards which limit the amount the interest rate on an ARM loan can change in an adjustment interval and/or over the life of the loan.
Joint Liability	Liability shared among two or more people, each of whom is liable for the full debt.
Joint Tenancy	A form of ownership of property giving each person equal interest in the property, including rights of survivorship.
Jumbo Loan	A mortgage larger than the $240,000 limit set by the Federal National Mortgage Association and the Federal Home Loan Mortgage Corporation.
Junior Mortgage	A mortgage subordinate to the claim of a prior lien or mortgage. In the case of a foreclosure, a senior mortgage or lien will be paid first.
Late Charge	Penalty paid by a borrower when a payment is made after the due date.
Legal Description	A means of identifying the exact boundaries of land.
Lender	The bank, mortgage company, or mortgage broker offering the loan.

LIBOR (London Interbank Offered Rate)	The interest rate charged among banks in the foreign market for short-term loans to one another. A common index for ARM loans.
Lien	A legal claim by one person on the property of another for security for payment of a debt.
Loan Application	An initial statement of personal and financial information required to apply for a loan.
Loan Application Fee	Fee charged by a lender to cover the initial costs of processing a loan application. The fee may include the cost of obtaining a property appraisal, a credit report, and a lock-in fee or other closing costs incurred during the process or the fee may be in addition to these charges.
Loan Origination Fee	Fee charged by a lender to cover administrative costs of processing a loan.
Loan-to-Value Ratio (LTV)	The percentage of the loan amount to the appraised value (or the sales price, whichever is less) of the property.
Lock or Lock-In	A lender's guarantee of an interest rate for a set period of time. The time period is usually that between loan application approval and loan closing. The lock-in protects you against rate increases during that time.
Margin	A specified percentage that is added to your chosen financial index to determine your new interest rate at the time of adjustment for ARM loans.
Mortgage	A written instrument, duly executed and delivered, that creates a lien upon real estate as security for the payment of a specific debt.
Mortgage Banker	An individual or company that originates and/or services mortgage loans.
Mortgage Broker	An individual or company that arranges financing for borrowers.

Mortgage Loan   A loan for which real estate serves as collateral to provide for repayment in case of default.

Mortgage Note   Legal document obligating a borrower to repay a loan at a stated interest rate during a specified period of time. The agreement is secured by a mortgage or deed of trust or other security instrument.

Mortgagee   The lender in a mortgage loan transaction.

Mortgagor   The borrower in a mortgage loan transaction.

Negative Amortization   A loan payment schedule in which the outstanding principal balance of a loan goes up rather than down because the payments do not cover the full amount of interest due. The monthly shortfall in payment is added to the unpaid principal balance of the loan.

Non-Assumption Clause   A statement in a mortgage contract forbidding the assumption of the mortgage by another borrower without the prior approval of the lender.

Note   Legal document obligating a borrower to repay a loan at a stated interest rate during a specified period of time. The agreement is secured by a mortgage or deed of trust or other security instrument.

Notice of Default   Written notice to a borrower that a default has occurred and that legal action may be taken.

Offer   The submittal of a set of terms for the purchase of real estate.

Origination Fee   Fee charged by a lender to cover administrative costs of processing a loan.

Partition   A division of real property among co-owners.

Payment Cap   Consumer safeguards which limit the amount monthly payments on an adjustable-rate mortgage may change. Since they do not limit the amount of interest the lender is earning, they may cause negative amortization.

Per Diem Interest   Interest calculated per day.

PITI   Abbreviation for Principal, Interest, Taxes and Insurance, the components of a monthly mortgage payment.

Power of Attorney   Legal document authorizing one person to act on behalf of another.

Pre-approval   The process of determining how much money a prospective homebuyer or refinancer will be eligible to borrow prior to application for a loan, including a preliminary review of a borrower's credit report.

Prepaid Expenses   Taxes, insurance and assessments paid in advance of their due dates.

Prepaid Interest   Interest that is paid in advance of when it is due which is typically charged to a borrower at closing to cover interest on the loan between the closing date and the first payment date.

Prepayment   Full or partial repayment of the principal before the contractual due date.

Prepayment Penalty   Fee charged by a lender for a loan paid off in advance of the contractual due date.

Pre-qualification   The process of determining how much money a prospective homebuyer will be eligible to borrow prior to application for a loan.

Principal   The amount of debt, not counting interest, left on a loan.

Private Mortgage Insurance (PMI)   Insurance to protect the lender in case you default on your loan, generally not required with conventional loans if the down payment is at least 20%.

Purchase Agreement   Contract signed by buyer and seller stating the terms and conditions under which a property will be sold.

Quitclaim Deed	A deed which conveys as much right, title and interest, if any, as the grantor may have in the property.
Real Estate	The land and all the things permanently attached to it.
Real Property	Real estate and the rights of ownership.
Recording	The process of filing of certain legal instruments or documents with the appropriate government office.
Reconveyance	The transfer of property back to the owner when a mortgage loan is fully repaid.
Recording	The act of entering documents concerning title to a property into the public records.
Referee's Deed	A deed given by a referee or other public officer pursuant to a court order for the sale of property.
Refinancing	The process of paying off one loan with the proceeds from a new loan secured by the same property.
RESPA	The Real Estate Settlement Procedures Act, a federal law that gives consumers the right to review information about loan settlement costs.
Right of Survivorship	The automatic succession to the interest of a deceased joint owner in a joint tenancy.
Right to Rescission	Under the provisions of the Truth-in-Lending Act, the borrower's right, on certain kinds of loans, to cancel the loan within three days of signing a mortgage.
Sales Agreement	Contract signed by buyer and seller stating the terms and conditions under which a property will be sold.

Second Mortgage   An additional mortgage placed on a property that has rights that are subordinate to the first mortgage.

Settlement   Also known as closing, refers to the conclusion of a real estate transaction and includes the delivery of the security instrument, signing of legal documents and the disbursement of the funds necessary to the sale of the home or loan transaction.

Settlement Costs   Also known as closing costs, refers to the costs for services that must be performed before the loan can be initiated, such as title fees, recording fees, appraisal fee, credit report fee, pest inspection, attorney's fees, and surveying fees.

Severalty   Ownership by a person in his own right.

Specific Performance   The requirement that a party must perform as agreed under a contract.

Statute of Frauds   Legal doctrine providing that all agreements concerning title to real estate must be in writing to be enforceable.

Survey   A measurement of land, prepared by a licensed surveyor, showing a property's boundaries, elevations, improvements, and relationship to surrounding tracts.

Sweat Equity   Value added to a property in the form of labor or services of the owner rather than cash.

Tax Impound   Money paid to and held by a lender for annual tax payments.

Tax Lien   Claim against a property for unpaid taxes.

Tax Sale   Public sale of property by a government authority as a result of non-payment of taxes.

Tenancy by the Entirety

An estate held by a husband and wife in which each have an undivided and equal right of possession during their joint lives, with the right of survivorship in the other spouse.

Tenancy in Common

An ownership of real estate by two or more persons, each of whom has an undivided fractional interest in the whole property, without any right of survivorship.

Term

The period of time between the beginning loan date on the legal documents and the date the entire balance of the loan is due.

Title

Document which gives evidence of ownership of a property. Also indicates the rights of ownership and possession of the property.

Title Company

A company that insures title to property.

Title Insurance

Refers to an insurance policy which protects the lender and/or buyer against loss due to disputes over ownership of a property.

Title Search

Examination of municipal records to ensure that the seller is the legal owner of a property and that there are no liens or other claims against the property.

Transfer Tax

Tax paid when title passes from one owner to another.

Truth-in-Lending Act

Federal law requiring written disclosure of the terms of a mortgage by a lender to a borrower after application.

Underwriting

In mortgage lending, the process of determining the risks involved in a particular loan and establishing suitable terms and conditions for the loan.

Usury

Interest charged in excess of the legal rate established by law.

VA Loans	Fixed-rate loans guaranteed by the U.S. Department of Veterans Affairs. They are designed to make housing affordable for eligible U.S. veterans. VA loans are available to veterans, reservists, active-duty personnel, and surviving spouses of veterans with 100% entitlement. Eligible veterans may be able to purchase a home with no down payment, no cash reserve, no application fee, and lower closing costs than other financing options.
Variable Rate	Interest rate that changes periodically in relation to an index.
Variance	The authorization to improve or develop a particular property in a manner not authorized by the zoning ordinance.
Verification of Deposit (VOD)	Document signed by the borrower's bank or other financial institution verifying the borrower's account balance and history.
Verification of Employment (VOE)	Document signed by the borrower's employer verifying the borrower's position and salary.
Waiver	Voluntary relinquishment or surrender of some right or privilege.
Walk-through	A final inspection of a home to check for problems that may need to be corrected before closing.

BIBLIOGRAPHY

Black's Law Dictionary, Fifth Edition. St. Paul, MN: West Publishing Company, 1979.

Basic Real Estate Law in New York. Eau Claire, WI: National Business Institute, Inc., 1991.

Black's Law Dictionary, Fifth Edition. St. Paul, MN: West Publishing Company, 1979.

Corley, Robert N., Shedd, Peter J. and Floyd, Charles F. *Real Estate and the Law*. New York, NY: Random House, 1982.

Gaudio, Arthur R. *Real Estate Brokerage Law*. St. Paul, MN: West Publishing Co., 1987.

Jennings, Marianne M.*Real Estate Law*. Boston, MA: Kent Publishing Company, 1985.

Quail, Beverly J.*Real Property Practice and Litigation*. Colorado Springs, CO: Shepards/McGraw Hill, Inc., 1990.

Randolph Jr., Patrick H.*Current Developments in Real Estate Law*. Chicago, IL: American Bar Association, Probates and Trust Law Section, 1992.

The United States Department of Housing and Urban Development (Date Visited: May 2000) [http:www.hud.gov].

Weinberg, Norman, Colletti, Paul J., Colavito, William A., and Melchior, Frank A.*Guide for the New York Real Estate Salesperson*. New York, NY: John Wiley & Sons, 1988.